*George Lindsay
and the Art of
Technical Analysis*

George Lindsay and the Art of Technical Analysis
Trading Systems of a Market Master

Ed Carlson

Vice President, Publisher: Tim Moore
Associate Publisher and Director of Marketing: Amy Neidlinger
Executive Editor: Jim Boyd
Editorial Assistant: Pamela Boland
Senior Marketing Manager: Julie Phifer
Assistant Marketing Manager: Megan Colvin
Cover Designer: Alan Clements
Managing Editor: Kristy Hart
Project Editor: Betsy Harris
Copy Editor: Cheri Clark
Proofreader: Water Crest Publishing, Inc.
Indexer: Lisa Stumpf
Compositor: Nonie Ratcliff
Manufacturing Buyer: Dan Uhrig

© 2012 by Pearson Education, Inc.
Publishing as FT Press
Upper Saddle River, New Jersey 07458

This book is sold with the understanding that neither the author nor the publisher is engaged in rendering legal, accounting, or other professional services or advice by publishing this book. Each individual situation is unique. Thus, if legal or financial advice or other expert assistance is required in a specific situation, the services of a competent professional should be sought to ensure that the situation has been evaluated carefully and appropriately. The author and the publisher disclaim any liability, loss, or risk resulting directly or indirectly, from the use or application of any of the contents of this book.

FT Press offers excellent discounts on this book when ordered in quantity for bulk purchases or special sales. For more information, please contact U.S. Corporate and Government Sales, 1-800-382-3419, corpsales@pearsontechgroup.com. For sales outside the U.S., please contact International Sales at international@pearson.com.

Company and product names mentioned herein are the trademarks or registered trademarks of their respective owners.

All rights reserved. No part of this book may be reproduced, in any form or by any means, without permission in writing from the publisher.

Printed in the United States of America

ISBN-10: 0-13-476994-5
ISBN-13: 978-0-13-476994-3

Pearson Education LTD.
Pearson Education Australia PTY, Limited
Pearson Education Singapore, Pte. Ltd.
Pearson Education North Asia, Ltd.
Pearson Education Canada, Ltd.
Pearson Educatión de Mexico, S.A. de C.V.
Pearson Education—Japan
Pearson Education Malaysia, Pte. Ltd.

Library of Congress Cataloging-in-Publication Data

Carlson, Ed, 1959-
  George Lindsay and the art of technical analysis : trading systems of a market master / Ed Carlson.
    p. cm.
  Includes bibliographical references and index.
  ISBN 978-0-13-269906-8 (hbk. : alk. paper)
  1. Lindsay, George, 1906-1987. 2. Technical analysis (Investment analysis) I. Title.
  HG4529.C3676 2012
  332.63'2042—dc23
                                       2011017617

This book is dedicated to my wife, Keika, for her patience and support during the writing of this book.

And to our young son, Edward Kazuya, whose big smile and glowing optimism brightened even the darkest days and who was always there to enthusiastically applaud even my most meager accomplishments.

Content

Introduction 1

Part I: Biography and "The Other History"

Chapter 1: Biography 7

Chapter 2: The Other History 23

Part II: Three Peaks and a Domed House

Chapter 3: The Phenomenon 39

Chapter 4: Three Peaks 49

Chapter 5: A Domed House 59

Chapter 6: The Tri-Day Method 79

Part III: The Lindsay Timing Model

Chapter 7: Overview of the Lindsay
Timing Model 93

Chapter 8: Key Dates 103

Chapter 9: The Low-Low-High Count 119

Chapter 10: Combining the Counts 129

Part IV: The Counts

Chapter 11: Long-Term Cycles and Intervals .. *143*

Chapter 12: Basic Movements *161*

*Chapter 13: Counts from the Middle
Section* *189*

Chapter 14: Case Study: The 1960s *203*

Glossary *227*

Index *235*

Acknowledgments

The Author would like to acknowledge and thank the following people for their help in providing the information necessary to make this book a reality. Their help ranged from personal recollections to providing actual research and correspondence from Lindsay. They are presented in alphabetical order.

Stephanie Cassidy
(Archivist, Art Students League of New York)

Phil Covato

Arch Crawford

Peter Eliades

Carl Futia

Yale Hirsch

Karen E. King
(Curator, National Public Broadcasting Archives)

Larry Pesavento

George Schade

Larry Williams

Jonathan Wood

Very special thanks are owed to the following people:

John Bollinger, who shared a treasure-trove of old Lindsay newsletters and correspondence. This would have been a very different book without those materials. Readers who have been exposed to Lindsay's writings only via the Investors Intelligence collection will find their worlds expanded significantly thanks to John's safeguarding of these materials.

Janice Teisch, widow of Stuart Teisch, Lindsay's partner. Janice shared her insider's view of the Lindsay organization. She also had a suitcase full of past reports, photos, and so on, which made a definite impact on this book.

Lastly, a very warm thank you is owed to the family of George Lindsay. Their support and encouragement for this book was second to none. Their intimate knowledge of a man, whom many described as a loner, provided insights which could have come from nowhere else. My thanks go to Vickie Lindsay Gilbert, Don Gilbert, Tamara Mitchell, and, most notably, James Lindsay, whose hours of work, e-mails, and phone calls could never receive their due praise.

Help was also obtained from the following organizations:

The CME Group

Investors Intelligence

To obtain a collection of George Lindsay articles, please contact

Investors Intelligence
30 Church St
New Rochelle, NY 10801
914-632-0422
www.investorsintelligence.com

All price charts were created in MetaStock, Equis.com.

About the Author

Ed Carlson, CMT, is an independent trader and consultant based in Seattle, Washington. He hosts the *MTA Podcast Series: Conversations* and manages the website *Seattle Technical Advisors.com*. Ed spent 20 years as a stockbroker; he is a chartered market technician and holds an M.B.A. from Wichita State University.

Introduction

"It has been proven time and time again that true and lasting success lies in the dissemination of knowledge, rather than in its concealment."[1]–R. N. Elliott, founder of Elliott Wave analysis

Who was George Lindsay and why did I undertake to write this book? If you've never heard of George Lindsay, you've already answered the second part of the question. Lindsay was considered a "stock guru" in the 1960s and 1970s. His market opinions often appeared in the *New York Times* next to other prognosticators whose names are more commonly known today, but very few people today are acquainted with Lindsay. Even among technical analysts who do know the name, very few are familiar with his work.

Lindsay's ideas are in danger of becoming lost to history. He never wrote a book on his market methods, only newsletters. He did write one book (*The Other History*, examined in Chapter 2) but it pertained to politics and history, not the markets. This book is the result of reviewing an untold number of his past newsletters and cobbling together the partial descriptions of his different models into coherent, step-by-step explanations.

It's no wonder that very few market participants have chosen to use his methods. Reading Lindsay's newsletters is like drinking from a fire hose. His style of writing is very difficult to read. The reader never gets a moment to "catch his breath" as the ideas just keep jumping off the page. The presentation format of his newsletters is difficult as well. Modern readers have become accustomed to the formatting of word processors—bullets, labeling, charts placed near the narrative, and so on. As I read Lindsay's newsletters, I imagined him sitting at a typewriter, typing to the right side of the page, reaching up with his left hand to shift the carriage back to start a new line, and blasting through yet another line, the ideas pouring forth with very little thought given to anyone trying to assimilate the mass of information being thrown at them.

We live in a world that would send the best and brightest of a generation off to fight and die for the invisible hand of Adam Smith, but ask those same people about technical analysis and they call it voodoo. Those who have accepted and practice technical analysis tend to gather into their own camps of like-mined analysis. Lindsay was an unintentional iconoclast. His approach, while often incorrectly described as cycles, was an original approach different from anything previously known. Like Lindsay's mother, who spent the majority of her acting career off-Broadway, Lindsay's ideas were decidedly "off-Wall Street." Modern technicians often seem to be spending more and more of their time examining the micro—30-minute charts, 5-minute charts, tick charts—an approach which, when taken to the extreme, is myopic and can border on nihilism. Lindsay took a broad, perhaps healthier, view of the market—but one that shouldn't be confused with anything approximating the buy-and-hold approach. While others may focus on the trees, Lindsay was busy mapping the forest.

It has been said that in order to understand the philosophy, one must understand the philosopher and his times. Never was this truer than in trying to understand the work of George Lindsay. Lindsay has been a mystery figure. Prior to this book, very little has been known about the man himself. Who was Lindsay? Genius or high-school dropout; artist or sophisticated Wall Street professional; heterosexual, homosexual, or asexual; a right-wing political conservative or a nonconformist dreamer and futurist? The answers to these questions come from an understanding of Lindsay's background and hence the biography in Chapter 1.

Lindsay's experience as an artist can be seen throughout his work in the markets. Charlie Parker, the great, early-twentieth-century jazz saxophonist, once said, "You've got to learn your instrument. Then, you practice, practice, practice. And then, when you finally get up there on the bandstand, forget all that and just wail." That's probably good advice when using the models Lindsay created. Like music, his models were full of rules and specific counts but the magic lay in the exceptions to those rules. It is by learning and practicing the guidelines laid out in this book that one can hope to achieve that proverbial "feel for the market" and "just wail."

Ed Carlson

March 2, 2011

Endnote

1. Robert Prechter, *R. N. Elliott's Masterworks*, 1980/1994/2005.

Part I

Biography and "The Other History"

Chapter 1: Biography   7

Chapter 2: The Other History   23

Chapter 1

Biography

"I can understand your feelings about New York, but I don't think I would be content anywhere else. I am single and unconventional and can breathe only in a big city." –George Lindsay

Family History

George Lindsay appears to be the fourth generation of the Lindsay family born in Virginia. George's paternal grandfather, Albert Loftus Lindsay, was an officer in the Confederate army during the American Civil War. In April 1862, Albert was made chief of General John Bankhead Magruder's signal corps. Albert's interest in codes and "secret messages" would one day manifest itself in George's passion for technical analysis.

George Lindsay's mother, Nellie Victoria Meyer Lindsay (b. 1876; d. 1954) was an actress in musical comedies, on and off Broadway, and used the stage name Nellie Victoria. A photo, dated 1903, of Nellie Victoria can be found in the Macauley's Theatre collection in the University of Louisville archives. Another photo of Nellie Victoria can be found in the University of Washington Libraries, Special Collections Division. Nellie Lindsay passed away on December 8, 1954.

George's father, George Sr. (b. 1863; d. 1921), studied engineering and graduated in 1882 from Virginia Tech. He was Chief Journal Clerk of the Virginia legislature for several decades. He was appointed Commissioner of Valuations for Norfolk, Virginia, on March 7, 1900, and served as the first head of the IRS in Norfolk, a position he held until his death in 1921.

George Lindsay was born November 11, 1906, in Portsmouth, Virginia, followed by his brother, Frank Loftus Lindsay, in 1910. The family home at 229 Mount Vernon Avenue in Portsmouth remains there today. At age 14, after the passing of his father, George was sent to the Pennington School in New Jersey, a boarding school 60 miles away from his remaining family, who moved to New York to be with Nellie's sister.

An interest in engineering ran deep in the Lindsay family. His mother's artistic talents were inherited by George as well. Inheriting these two very different attributes not only made for the perfect background to Lindsay's later interest in technical analysis but surely contributed to his unique approach.

Artist

By the fall of 1927, at 21 years of age (see Figure 1.1), George was enrolled in the Art Students League of New

York. The school boasts an impressive list of alumni including Georgia O'Keeffe, Jackson Pollock, and Roy Lichtenstein.

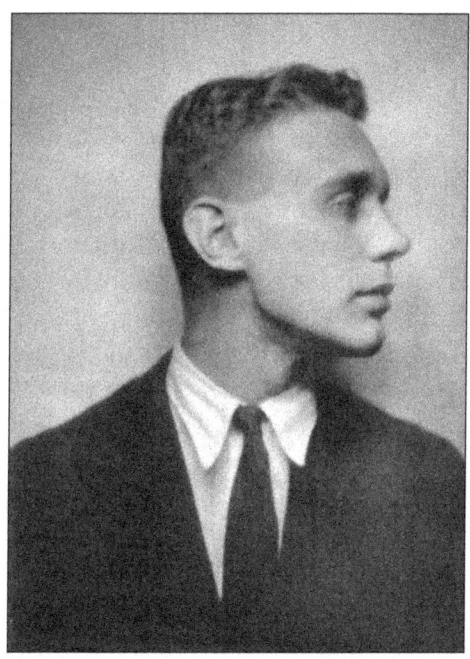

FIGURE 1.1 *George at 21 years of age. (Source: Lindsay family)*

Lindsay became involved with one of the heavyweights in the advertising business at that time, James Yates. Family members recount that George was involved with a redesign of the Camel cigarette pack in the 1930s. He even had his brother, Frank, draw the parallel lines on the pyramids. It is well-documented that James Yates, while art director at William Esty, handled the Camel Cigarette account, so a connection between the two men is clear. Yates eventually became Art Director for *The Saturday Evening Post*. By 1933, George was working as a commercial artist for Macy's Department Stores.

Despite the consensus view of those who knew him later in life that George was a homosexual, it is known that he did propose marriage to a woman in 1931. George never opened up to anyone as to what went wrong in the relationship or why she turned him down. Late in her life, Nellie would tell others that in the 1930s George would stay in his room by himself and play the Victrola, laugh, and "have a grand time all alone." As others would recount in the future, George was not a talkative man. Yet, despite these "quirks," George was personable and always available to answer questions about his work.

Chicago

No one knows for certain when Lindsay developed his interest in the markets or his unique ideas and approach. But on June 1, 1939, George paid $1,475 for a seat on the Chicago Board of Trade (see Figure 1.2), so it can be assumed that he had been intently working on some of his ideas by then and was looking for a way to test them. A year later, after Germany invaded Paris on June 14, 1940, trading at the CBOT came to a virtual standstill. As will be shown in Chapter 2, "The Other History," George had an immense knowledge of history and could probably see that the immediate future at the CBOT was bleak. That would explain why, on June 12, 1940, he had already sold his seat on the exchange. He was paid $1,300 for it.

FIGURE 1.2   *George in front of the Chicago Board of Trade in 1939. (Source: Lindsay family)*

Los Angeles

A month earlier, Frank had moved to Los Angeles in search of work. It wouldn't have taken much to persuade an unemployed George and Nellie to leave the cold New York winters and move to warm and sunny Los Angeles. The 1944 voter rolls show George and Nellie both registered as Republicans and living in an apartment building in Hollywood. George continued to live with Nellie until her death.

George wrote that he studied aircraft engineering at the University of Southern California at the outbreak of WWII and then worked as an engineer for McDonnell Douglas during the period 1942–45. He couldn't have been at USC for long because he was still in Chicago in mid-1940 and began his employment at Douglas Aircraft in 1942.

George was part of a massive hiring boom at Douglas Aircraft. World War II meant good times for Douglas. But the company suffered at the end of hostilities. The Douglas Aircraft Co. was forced to cut its workforce by 100,000 people at the end of the war. No doubt, an artist with little in the way of an engineering background was among those to be let go. There is no record of George being employed after his time at Douglas Aircraft. It is thought that by this time George couldn't handle the pressure and frustration involved in working with others.

He wrote his pamphlet "An Aid to Timing" in 1950 and founded his advisory service in 1951. By the 1950s, George was itching to get back to New York but was needed to stay in California to take care of Nellie, who had developed breast cancer. It is thought that George preferred the cold climate of New York to the balmy breezes of Southern California. It is well-known that in later years in New York, George would keep a window open during the winter. According to family members, the time surrounding Nellie's death and the role George played as her primary caregiver was George's "shining hour." After Nellie's death, George left Los Angeles to return to New York in 1955.

The Analyst

Quite a legend has grown up around George Lindsay. Yale Hirsch, in the *Stock Trader's Almanac*, wrote, "George Lindsay is one of the few people in the world who from memory can reproduce a chart of stock market prices for every one of the last 150 years." Lindsay (see Figure 1.3) was a "unique" individual. He was often called eccentric, a loner, peculiar, seemingly bizarre, brilliant, and a typical "Greenwich Village Bohemian." And yet he has been described just as many times as sharing, modest, open, kind and generous, not materialistic, having a desire to help others, a very sharing person, and willing to admit to being incorrect—two sets of personality traits that are difficult to reconcile.

His last residence, 720 Greenwich Street in Greenwich Village, was a studio apartment that had a separate bathroom (the water continually dripping from the bathroom tap) and a small kitchen with swinging doors, though he rarely cooked for himself. He slept on a convertible sofa in the main room and did most of his work on a card table there. He had one small bookcase. A poster on his wall, of a naked Venus in a clamshell, he had found on the sidewalk in someone's trash. Lindsay didn't even own a television. The ceiling in his apartment was very high and there was a big window that he would keep open even in the winter.

FIGURE 1.3   *George circa 1960s. (Source: Lindsay family)*

Lindsay was nocturnal so he worked nights. He had a strange living pattern which included breakfast at 3:00 a.m. He never got around to buying dress shirts, and his entire supply came from his sister-in-law, Mary, and niece, Vickie, in California. Despite this lack of interest in clothing and his immediate surroundings, Lindsay was known to be a very vain individual. He had at least two face-lifts during his life. Unfortunately, the last face-lift left him a bit strange in appearance as it pushed up his eyebrows so he looked perpetually surprised or as if his eyebrows might have been burned off.

He also wore a toupee. At one time he owned three: one to look as though he had just had a haircut, one to look as though he needed a haircut, and one to appear as a "normal" length.

Political Views

In February of 1970, Ralph Nader announced the formation of Campaign GM. The campaign's goals included convincing GM's large institutional shareholders to force GM to "make a larger commitment to solving such problems as air pollution, highway safety, and job opportunities for minorities."[1]

Four days after the defeat of Campaign GM's proposal at the 1971 shareholders' meeting, Lindsay felt the need to write the following in his May 28th newsletter:

"The central idea of Ralph Nader's organization is that various groups should be represented in management—for example, consumers, ethnic minorities, dealers, workers, etc. This goes under the general heading of 'consumerism' today, but it is straight out of fascism. Not the fascism that we remember from Hitler, but the original doctrine as introduced by Mussolini in 1922. And General Motors continues under assault on the grounds that it is too big. This, of course, is an essentially socialistic idea."[2]

From this small insight into Lindsay's thinking, and his California voter registration as a Republican, it can be inferred that his politics were decidedly right-wing, conservative. The modern reader will find Lindsay's politics to be yet another incongruous personality trait of his as the consensus opinion of Lindsay during his New York years was that he was a homosexual. Lindsay is described by his fellow analysts at that time as flamboyant, flaming, a nonstop talker, delightful, and exhilarating. Lindsay must have cut quite a figure with his bright red wig, black patent leather boots, blue double-breasted blazer, and a striped shirt sent by California relatives. In a letter to fellow technician James Alphier (October 18, 1971), Lindsay wrote, *"I am single and unconventional and can breathe only in a big city."*[3]

Advisory Service

Lindsay founded his advisory service while still in California in 1951, and it lasted until 1975. He wrote a weekly investment letter he called *George Lindsay's Opinion*. In February 1972, at 65 years of age, Lindsay went to a monthly format. Lindsay maintained his advisory service until 1975 and after that wrote four letters a year as part of John Brown's *The Advisor,* which was published in Houston, Texas. In 1979, he became a consultant with Ernst & Company, which took over the production of the newsletter, still based on Lindsay's analyses. He stopped publishing the newsletter in 1984. Lindsay did not trade for his own account. His love was the research he was doing, and by 1969 his primary research did not concern the markets. Rather, he had discovered "intervals" in history and was certain he had discovered a way to predict historical events. In 1971, he presented his ideas at the first international conference of the World Future Society in Washington, D.C.

He also made several presentations on his discovery to a New York organization he belonged to called S.I.R.E., the Society for Investigation of Recurring Events. His ideas are presented in detail in the next chapter.

Stuart Teisch

Stuart Teisch is a name that appeared on the byline of Lindsay's newsletter next to Lindsay's own name. Teisch was the other half of the Lindsay organization and had a 17-year association with Lindsay. Stuart Teisch was born April 29, 1929. A native New Yorker, he studied podiatry at Long Island University and was a practicing podiatrist by the time he discovered technical analysis. Technical analysis soon became Teisch's passion, and he gave up his medical practice to fully immerse himself in the markets. Teisch's family were even part of the organization: His mother acted as the company's bookkeeper, and his father and Teisch's wife, Janice, both helped with the day-to-day operations of the business.

When Lindsay retired in the 1970s, Stuart and Janice moved to Arizona, where he started a phone advisory service and newsletter. In his later years, Teisch worked for Charles Schwab. Stuart Teisch passed away on March 30, 1998, in Scottsdale, Arizona.

Track Record

By 1980, Lindsay's admirers were legion and his detractors were few. The race for first among equals, in the eyes of the public, however, allows for only one champion. At that time, the cup went to Joe Granville, the

Kansas City technician famous for his On Balance Volume indicator. Granville was known as a great showman who would emerge from a coffin at an investment conference, or appear to walk across water (at a swimming pool) when meeting clients.

While a comparison to Granville was hardly the kind of thing Lindsay would have appreciated, he must have known he had reached a rarified level in the eyes of the public when the analyst James Alphier published a report in 1981 titled "Granville in Perspective." In it he summarized Granville's record. He then compared it to the records of the few market analysts who were true market gurus because of their long records of successful predictions. Listed among those gurus was Lindsay.

Alphier wasn't the only one to take note of Lindsay. Yale Hirsch, publisher of the *Stock Trader's Almanac*, had taken an interest in Lindsay, as well. In 1968, the *Almanac* began publishing Lindsay's annual forecast and continued doing so for over a decade. In the 1968 *Stock Trader's Almanac*, Yale Hirsch wrote: "Many annual forecasts are published each January by leading Wall Street analysts. One unusual forecaster who has attempted the impossible during the past ten years is George Lindsay, editor of *George Lindsay's Opinion*. Each year he predicts the course of the stock market for a whole year, on a month-to-month basis, pinpointing rallies and declines and estimating the price range of the Dow Jones industrial average." The *Stock Trader's Almanac* called Lindsay's 1969 forecast "the finest long-term forecast we have ever seen."

In 1987, John Brown, who had merged the Lindsay letter into his own, published a letter from Lindsay dated July 1, 1987. Lindsay died shortly thereafter but not before communicating his feelings to Brown that *"it now seems likely that the last high will come some time in August 1987."* On August 25th, the Dow started what appeared to be a normal correction but one that morphed into one of the biggest Wall Street crashes in history as it fell over 40% during the next 39 trading days to an intraday low on October 20, 1987.

Wall Street Week with Louis Rukeyser

Lindsay appeared twice on Louis Rukeyser's television program *Wall Street Week*—once on October 16, 1981, and again on May 8, 1983. *Wall Street Week* was produced by Maryland Public Television and was the first nationally syndicated television show to focus on Wall Street. The show ran for 32 years before Rukeyser left in 2002.

An inside joke among family members was that because George didn't like coats and ties, the only dress shirt he had available to wear on the program by that time had a hole in the left shoulder.

During his last appearance on the program, onlookers commented that Lindsay struggled to get to the stage and had to be helped.

Years later, during an episode featuring snippets of past guests and highlighting each guest's forecasting ability, Rukeyser said, "In October 1981, eight months before history's greatest bull market began, I interviewed a seemingly bizarre guest, who turned out to be an uncannily accurate forecaster." During his first appearance on the program in October of 1981,

Rukeyser had asked Lindsay, "When do we get out of this bear market and into that bull market?" Lindsay replied, *"The end of the bear market—the earliest I can count it is about August 26, 1982. I think 750 to 770 is more like the range of the final low."*

The intraday low of the bear market occurred on August 9, 1982, and the closing low, three days later, was at 776.92.

Death

Lindsay's obituary in the New York Times states that he died of a heart attack on August 6, 1987. George's marker is at Oak Hill Memorial Park in San Jose, California, where his ashes are interred.

Conclusion

No one's life can be summed up in just a few words. The objective of this chapter is not only to document Lindsay's unusual ability to time the market but also to provide some understanding of the personal history that produced that ability. When drawing a picture, one difference between the artist and nonartist is the way in which they look at the blank page before them. The nonartist often begins by drawing an object, in detail, in one area of the page and then moving on to another detailed object in a different area. An artist, on the other hand, will think in terms of the entire page and use broad, sweeping motions unafraid, almost uninterested, in the details of the figures until the broad sketch is completed. This approach is vividly clear in Lindsay's approach to the markets and is very different from most approaches to technical analysis today.

Endnotes

1. *Science,* May 29, 1970, Vol. 168 no. 3935, pp. 1077–1078.

2. Unless otherwise indicated, all quotes in this chapter are taken from George Lindsay's self-published newsletter, *George Lindsay's Opinion,* during the years 1959–72.

3. George Lindsay, letter to James Alphier, October 18, 1971.

Chapter 2

The Other History

"*Everything in the universe moves in a rhythm. Nothing happens at random. The underlying factors are, in their turn, subject to the same rhythms as the final product. The whole is not the sum of the parts, but both the whole and parts labor under similar influences.*"[1]
–George Lindsay

It is widely known that Lindsay's greatest passion was the subject matter in his book, *The Other History*, which he called "technical history." Lindsay coined the term (an allusion to technical analysis) to describe the methods explained in this book.

The Other History was Lindsay's only book. It is not known whether he attempted to go through normal publishing channels, but in the end he self-published the book through Vantage Publishing, a "subsidy" publisher. In other words, he paid to have it published.

For a writer whose subject matter was difficult and writing style dense, Lindsay's book, *The Other History*, must be, unfortunately, the most impenetrable example of his writing. Jampacked with minute details and obscure references, the book leaves the reader to determine for himself whether Lindsay was grasping at straws to build his case for "technical history" or whether he was actually on to something.

"Herodotus died 2400 years ago, but his influence is still pervasive. Every historical work since his day has, with rare exceptions, adhered to the model he set up. It has been a straight narrative of events in chronological order; to the extent that the author tried to explain them at all, he relied on accepted notions of cause and effect."

Lindsay wrote that only 20 books had been written over the previous century in this genre. He mentions as notable Dupuy's *Origine des tous les cultes*, *Historionomie* by Stromer von Reichenbach, and *Les rhythmes dans l'historie* by Gaston Georgel, adding that his book is in the school of Georgel. He also notes that very little has been written on the subject in English other than *The Law of Civilization and Decay* by Brooks Adams and *The Rule of Phase Applied to History* by Henry Adams. It is safe to assume that Lindsay developed these ideas himself as an outgrowth of his market timing techniques.

No number of examples can serve to convince the skeptical mind of Lindsay's ideas. But the mind is much more open to "technical history" after a review of Lindsay's market timing techniques, which also include the concept of time intervals. The skeptical are advised to reread this chapter after finishing the remainder of the book.

Time Intervals

The Other History, like Lindsay's work in the stock market, is concerned with intervals of time. The starting point is always an agitation: *"An agitation is a heightened consciousness and increased activity among a large number of people at a specific moment in time. It is normally directed toward a certain end. An agitation may be physical in nature, in which case it usually involves bloodshed; or it may be intellectual or emotional."* The important numbers to be acquainted with are 36, 40, and 56. These are intervals of time—36 years, 40 years, and 56 years. Each interval is a point estimate; Lindsay allows for a year on either side of the point estimate, so 36 years is the name of an interval that actually ends anywhere from 35 to 37 years after the starting point, or agitation. The same applies to 40 and 56. A final interval involves the years 64–69. What happens in the interim, between interval dates, is irrelevant and may be ignored.

These intervals mark times of ease or success after the initial difficulties associated with the starting point or time of agitation. *"According to the theory, any collective undertaking fails, or succeeds imperfectly, unless there was an agitation directed toward the same end about 36 or 40 years previously, and unless the central idea behind the effort was clearly defined at roughly the same time."* The first interval to occur after an agitation varies. It may be 36 years (35–37 years) or 40 years (39–41 years). As a side note, this book was begun in the 41st year after the publication of *The Other History*.

Often there is a retrograde movement. The retrograde movement is an attempt to turn back the clock which runs counter to the main trend of **difficult to easy.** *"It always appears shortly before the moment of final triumph, and confuses the outlook."* The retrograde movement normally appears shortly before the expiration of 40 years. The next interval is that of 56 years (55–57 years) and after that, the final interval of 64–69 years.

Wars and Unsuccessful Revolts

"...throughout history, the misfortune at an interval after an unsuccessful revolt has normally taken the form of a military reversal, the death of a sovereign, the end of a dynasty, or a combination of these."

An agitation of a physical nature that Lindsay spends a fair amount of time discussing is that of unsuccessful revolts. These intervals are looked upon from the view of the successful sovereign. Repercussions after the standard interval tend to hurt the party in power that had suppressed the revolt. Consequently, the intervals are described as easy (suppression of the rebellion) to difficult ("victory" for the rebels). *"According to my theory, the losers of unsuccessful revolts gain their ends, to some degree at least, after the lapse of one or more of the three intervals."*

A well-known example of an unsuccessful revolt is the American Civil War, 1861–65. It is also an example of multiple cycles overlapping and exerting their effects. When viewed as a simple rebellion, the progression goes from easy to difficult.

"Not only does the party which puts down the rebellion suffer misfortune after the lapse of an interval; the losing side usually achieves at least part of its aims." Of all the aims of the South during this time, the most infamous was to keep African-Americans in subjugation. In May of 1896, 35 years after the start of the Civil War, the Supreme Court of the United States handed down a decision in the case of *Plessy v Ferguson* that upheld the constitutionality of state laws requiring racial segregation under the doctrine of "separate but equal."

In September of 1901, 40 years after the beginning of the Civil War, President McKinley was shot and killed. McKinley was the leader of the side that had quelled the revolt. Lindsay wrote that in deciding whether there will be recognizable effects from assassination attempts, we must examine whether the counts agree with intervals from other agitations and gauge the impression an attempted assassination makes on contemporaries.

Finally, 56 years after 1861, Germany announced its policy of unrestricted submarine warfare (January 1917), forcing the United States into World War I. Again, one might think that America, being at a moment of difficulty, would lose the war. Not only was America at a juncture of both difficulty and ease, but Germany found itself at a juncture of difficulty.

"We have seen that two developments can normally be detected at the intervals after an unsuccessful revolt. The rebels, or their successors, gain a portion of what they had struggled for. Sometimes they realize the original aim in a positive fashion; in other cases, the best they can do is, in effect, wreak vengeance on the party

that suppressed the revolt. The faction which quelled the disturbance, or its lineal successor, suffers a misfortune in its turn. It may be particularized in a head of state, someone close to him, or an individual to whom he has delegated powers. On other occasions, the disaster is visited on the nation as a unit, and it has most often taken the form of a military defeat at the hands of a foreign power. When misfortune does not come in this obvious way, it is likely to come in that field or endeavor at which the winners of the earlier contest have tried hardest to succeed."

An excellent example of different progressions overlapping can be seen in 18th- and early-19th-century Germany. A period of difficult to easy (from the viewpoint of the German states) began with the defeat of Prussia, by Napoleon, in 1806 at the Battle of Jena. The 57-year interval in 1863 appeared to mark a turn in fortunes and culminated in the establishment of the German empire in 1871, 69 years after the Battle of Jena. The year 1871 marked the start of another count of 64–69 years of positive time. Count the 69-year interval from the establishment of the German empire in 1871 and you come to 1940. Hitler reached his apogee with the defeat of France in June 1940, and his fortunes began to wane when he lost the Battle of Britain that fall. At the same time, a progression of easy to difficult was occurring. Nationalistic revolts had occurred in both Berlin and Vienna in 1848. Both revolts were put down, starting a period of **easy to difficult** for German authorities. Then, 69 years later was the end of World War I, a period of difficulty that was offset somewhat by the period of ease that was to culminate in 1940.

Emotional Agitations

"The intervals may be counted, not only from episodes of violence, but from eruptions of an emotional nature."

An emotional agitation may be religious, economic, or political in nature. *"An emotional agitation is normally a juncture of difficulty, and the interval progresses from difficult to easy."* It is hard to date the genesis of an emotional agitation accurately. The starting point is not nearly as clear as bloodshed in a revolution or other physical agitation. Emotional agitations have an idiosyncrasy that Lindsay described: *"While the delayed effect after a physical agitation is largely confined to the country where the violence occurred, the repercussions following an emotional outburst can leap across national boundaries."* He found that these repercussions were most likely to spread if one or more conditions were met. If the agitation were based in an important locus of culture, such as 15th-century Florence, Italy, the effects were more likely to spread across borders. Lindsay wrote that the intensity of an agitation, more than its content, is a key factor. Finally, if the event was radically different from the accepted order of things, it was likely to spread regardless of borders. Another idiosyncrasy: *"As a rule, though not invariably, success for an idea is achieved after the second emotional agitation of a series directed toward the same end."*

The founding of the Christian church can be thought to have dated from the crucifixion of Jesus Christ.

Lindsay wrote, *"The ministry of Jesus Christ was an emotional agitation and the crucifixion was a purge."*

Lindsay wrote, *"Since the crucifixion is classified as a purge, the progression runs from easy to difficult; both Rome and the Jews were due to undergo misfortune."* This progression is from the viewpoint of the Romans and Jews. Using A.D. 30 as the most probable date of the crucifixion, counting forward 36 years to the year A.D. 66 saw the Jews revolt against Roman rule. Vespasian laid siege to Jerusalem in A.D. 68, and the city fell to Titus in August–September of A.D. 70 at the 40-year interval after the purge, or crucifixion.

The Romans suffered misfortunes too. If A.D. 30 was definitely the year of the crucifixion, then the Great Fire of Rome, in A.D. 64, was one year too early to be attributed to the progression from easy to difficult. But given the relative uncertainty of the date A.D. 30, the Great Fire of Rome deserves mention. The fire burned for five-and-a-half days and only 1 of 14 districts of Rome escaped the fire. Lindsay writes: *"The one that could have been predicted was the death of Nero in June 68, and even more typically, the extinction of the Julian-Claudian house. The repercussions in the case were more extraordinary than usual, for three emperors swiftly followed Nero in the 'long but single year,' as Tacitus called it."*

Lindsay wrote, *"Count the 55-year interval from the crucifixion in A.D. 30 and you come to 85. A bitter quarrel broke out between Emperor and Senate when Domitian had himself appointed censor for life."* The climax was reached at the 66-year interval in September of A.D. 96 when Domitian was assassinated.

As for the opposite progression, from difficult to easy, Lindsay wrote, "*The 64–69-year interval from difficult to easy after an important emotional agitation has normally signaled a period of remarkable prestige or progress. Sometimes this count denotes the start of such an era. In that case, the good fortune lasts another 64–69 years, and this may be stretched to 80 or 90 years under certain circumstances—when for example there is second agitation to count from.*"

To sum up, Lindsay explained his views best when he wrote: "*Emotional agitations are not the cause of subsequent success, but merely an outward sign of little understood forces which operate under the surface.*"..."*Arguments are never won by logic, merit or even performance: men are incapable of judging such points objectively.*"..."*The intervals operate by influencing the mind of a man in solitude no less than by arousing the crowd through the overworked bogey of "mass psychology.*"

Creative Concentrations

"*The chief requirement of this phenomenon is the appearance of a number of books or art within a brief time. The shorter the span in which they are bunched, the more valid the concentration is.*"

Another agitation is the Creative Concentration, a date surrounded by a concentration of great works of art. A Creative Concentration can include books, paintings, controversial plays, and music including symphonies and operas. Creative Concentrations always move from easy to difficult. Another feature of a creative concentration is that the merit of the books is recognized abroad as at home. Influence is what counts, not worth. Not every agitation is followed by repercussions at all three intervals. Some counts are more important than others. To estimate which, correlate the intervals of one country with those of its rivals. When ease and difficulty are scheduled for the same time (when two opposing intervals expire at the same time), it is unknown which will take effect first. Expect rapid shifts in fortune. Remember; disasters are momentary while stretches of prosperity last longer.

Lindsay gives the Enlightenment as a prime example of a Creative Concentration and dates it to 1749 based on a number of books which appeared around that year. Forty years later, a difficulty would be expected for France and, indeed, 1789 was the year of the French Revolution.

Einstein's *Annus Mirabilis* papers, *"a seminal exposition of a new principle in physics,"* published in 1905, together with a host of other German writers, formed a concentration that year. Forty years later marked the defeat of Germany in World War II.

"The technical historian is not afraid of coupling ideas from unrelated categories. He does not reject continuity of thought, but the connection need not be the obvious one that seems appropriate to the sentient mind. The meaningful thought is that which has been transformed, and perhaps rechanneled, through a period of subconscious rumination. It becomes an ingrained attitude rather than a directed effort."

The Lost Manuscripts

It is known that Lindsay was working on a second book at the time of his death. He had mentioned the work to people, and a partial manuscript has been discovered by family members. This book was to address time intervals of a much longer duration than the intervals Lindsay identified in his earlier work.

Lindsay developed what he called the M-Pattern of history (see Figure 2.1). He wrote that the method would not predict actual events, but rather, *"A way has been found however, to forecast the conditions which make a certain type of event probable at a given time."*[2] In the case of wars, his method would not predict that a war would occur, only which side was the likely winner. This assumes events within certain periods.

"There is no sure way of deciding that a specific event of prime importance will take place, such as a war between the major powers. If such a development is coming at all, however, the record implies that it will occur at one of the time periods which are calculable in advance."[3]

When projecting international events, the timing of one country must be synchronized with that of another, and the two governments must have unusual relations within this time period—that is, relations that go beyond the routine.

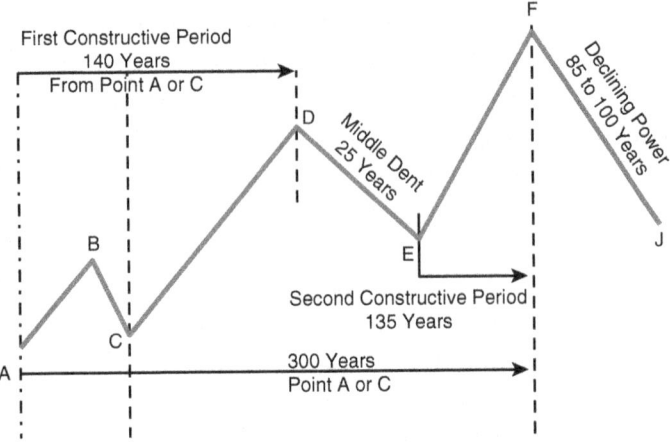

FIGURE 2.1 M-Pattern.

Conclusion

In his book, *The Other History*, Lindsay challenges the accepted views of "cause and effect" and replaces them with his own observations of time intervals. Like his market timing techniques, Lindsay's approach to history, although similar to cycles, is far more unique. It would be easy to dismiss the ideas presented in *The Other History* if it were not for the success Lindsay experienced using this same approach in predicting the stock market, another task many believe to be impossible. This chapter provides only a taste of Lindsay's book for the reader. In the original text, Lindsay's attempt to provide enough examples to be convincing unfortunately becomes overwhelming. *The Other History* is out of print but can be found in some library collections, including the M.T.A. Library.

Endnotes

1. Unless otherwise indicated, all quotes in this chapter are taken from George Lindsay's self-published book, *The Other History*, 1969.

2. George Lindsay, "A Way to Predict the Future" (unpublished manuscript; date [post-1982] unknown).

3. Ibid.

Part II

Three Peaks and a Domed House

Chapter 3: The Phenomenon   39

Chapter 4: Three Peaks   49

Chapter 5: A Domed House   59

Chapter 6: The Tri-Day Method   79

Chapter 3

The Phenomenon

"There are also periods when trends are short-lived and subject to frequent reversal. Technicians assume that such irregular markets do not follow any recognizable pattern for long and that abrupt changes in trend cannot be predicted. My studies show that these apparently haphazard movements nearly always follow the same pattern. The two formations to be explained have been repeated over and over again from the earliest records. A rough tally indicates that the market has followed them at least 60% of the time for the past 150 years."[1]
–George Lindsay

After introducing the concept in 1968, George Lindsay published his "Three Peaks and a Domed House" newsletter in 1970. This newsletter, along with others, later appeared in a book titled *Encyclopedia of Stock Market Techniques,* published by Investors Intelligence.

Those who are already familiar with this model will notice something missing from this book: Lindsay's numbering system for the different waves within the formation. The system Lindsay used in his 1970 newsletter explaining the "Three Peaks and a Domed House" was cumbersome and distracted from a student's understanding of the model. Even Lindsay didn't hold the system he used in that newsletter sacrosanct because only two years later, in his May 15, 1972, newsletter, he changed the system to include fewer numbers. This book has eliminated the numbering system entirely and replaced it with terms that should be intuitively obvious to the reader rather than forcing the reader to constantly check and recheck which numbers apply to which parts of the model.

Lindsay had a very definite opinion as to which equity index should be used with his model. In his 1969 pamphlet, "One Year Later: A Follow-Up of the Three Peaks and Domed House," Lindsay writes, *"Averages composed of a small number of blue chips have always had crisper chart patterns than all-inclusive indexes. It is largely because unseasoned stocks are in a state of flux: new ones are being added, old ones are dropped, and the number of shares is constantly changing. The Dow Jones stocks are more stable in composition. Talk of the Dow Jones Average as being unrepresentative is beside the mark. If you want to know the true level of 'the market,' look at the broader averages. If you want to predict the future, go by the Dow or the New York Times Industrials. Indeed, some technicians get the most reliable results by using an index of only ten or twelve sensitive and influential stocks. The NYSE Index of all stocks is nearly worthless in forecasting."*

This chapter's opening quote from Lindsay contains the bold statement (Lindsay was prone to such statements), *"A rough tally indicates that the market has followed them at least 60% of the time for the past 150 years."* Clearly 60% of the Dow's price action for the past 150 years was not spent forming the "Three Peaks and a Domed House" pattern. Lindsay's contention was that the pattern could be found at 60% of bull market tops and at the peaks of rallies in bear markets (cyclical bull markets). *"The majority of all major advances ended in a pattern which resembled the Three Peaks and a Domed House. Some came closer to the ideal form than others. However, a few top areas don't fit into the pattern at all: it would be stretching the imagination to see it around the highs of 1909 and 1937."* One hundred-fifty years prior to the year of publication of Lindsay's newsletter would have meant 1820—well before the Dow Jones Industrial Average was created in 1896 (and even before its forerunner, the *Dow Jones Averages,* was created and published by Charles Dow in 1884). Lindsay wrote, *"The Dow-Jones 20-stock average is used before 1897, the Dow-Jones Industrials since then."* The Dow-Jones 20-stock average is the Dow Railroad index, which, by 1896, contained 20 railroad stocks and evolved from the original *Dow Jones Averages* and its 11 transportation-related stocks. In Lindsay's 1965 newsletter "A Timing Method for Traders," Lindsay wrote that he used a daily average of seven market leaders from 1861 to 1885. That still leaves 41 years unaccounted for, but the examples Lindsay shares are no earlier than 1890.

Identifying Characteristics

Lindsay wrote that the two patterns which began July 26, 1893, and July 26, 1910, were very clear and provided the inspiration for the "Three Peaks and a Domed House" formation. These two patterns peaked September 4, 1895, and September 30, 1912, respectively. This chapter introduces the "Three Peaks and a Domed House" formation (subsequently referred to as 3PDh) and its major characteristics. These characteristics should not be passed by too quickly by the reader in search of more depth or detail because these characteristics, though simple, are extremely important. The pattern is ostensibly a method for identifying the end of a bull market. However, 3PDh is broader in scope than simply using it to find the top of a bull market. Once it's recognized, one can trade it on the way up, too. Identifying and separating true 3PDh patterns from imposters is essential to profitable trading of the pattern prior to its completion. Lindsay wrote: *"These patterns last a long time so anyone can use them to advantage if he recognizes them at an early stage."*

Lindsay also wrote, *"Through a very complicated procedure, it is possible to forecast the inception of such a movement before it begins."* Unfortunately, he didn't describe that "complicated procedure" and, unless he passed it on orally, it appears he took it with him to his grave. Fortunately, by identifying the key characteristics of the pattern, one needn't use complicated procedures to recognize the pattern long before its completion. The beauty of the pattern is in its simplicity.

Figure 3.1 presents an idealized shape of the 3PDh price pattern. One can clearly see the three peaks toward the left side of the figure followed by a sharp, three-wave sell-off. The Domed House encompasses everything after the three-wave sell-off (middle to right side of Figure 3.1), including the large sell-off taking prices back to the bottom of the entire 3PDh pattern. The chief characteristic of the whole chart is that price makes rapid upside progress, but continues for only a short time. In between the brief spurts, prices go through long stretches of consolidation, or sideways movements. The pattern is characterized by sharp rises followed by long consolidations. When you're searching for the pattern, it is tempting to accept advances that clearly break down into advancing waves rather than the sharp advances Lindsay described. Don't be tempted by these advancing "waves" unless other segments of the pattern are absolutely 3PDh and the weight of the evidence is undeniable. Whenever the market spends lots of time moving sideways, we should look for other indications of a 3PDh pattern. In this pattern, prices advance only about half the time—they move sideways on as many days as they advance.

FIGURE 3.1   *Idealized shape.*

Lindsay wrote: "*Both the Three Peaks and the Domed House are distinguished by the advances and declines which travel many points in a straight line. But these movements don't last long. In between the few explosive moves, the market spends much of the time backing and filling in a comparatively narrow range. These characteristics usually make it easy to recognize a formation shortly after it begins. Once the formation is underway, it usually lasts a long time. This gives it predictive value.*"

Lindsay differentiated between patterns that emerge from advances off a bear market low (capping a cyclical bull market) and those that culminate a secular bull market.

"*The most typical Three Peak-Domed House formations start at a bear market low. When this has been true, the highest point in the pattern has never equaled the top of the previous major bull market.*"

Lindsay didn't mean to imply that the 3PDh formations are any more common off of bear market lows than bull market highs. He only meant that formations which emerge from advances off bear market lows have a more "typical" structure (see Chapter 4, "Three Peaks," and Chapter 5, "A Domed House") than what one sees in patterns at bull market highs. Hence the following quotes:

"*The Three Peak-Domed House pattern can also begin in the course of a long advance. When this happens, the top of the Domed House is usually the bull market high.*"

"The patterns which start in the latter part of a major bull market do not normally last as long as those that begin at a bear market low and are often less symmetrical."

Finally, the completed Domed House section of the pattern should have a square effect about it and a rounded top. In Figure 3.1, after the Three Peaks at the left side of the chart, and after the three-wave sell-off, a small base is formed. This base is the first section of the Domed House and is followed by a sharp rise, which is called the First Floor Wall.

This First Floor Wall is followed by a five-wave reversal pattern that serves to consolidate the sharp rise. The five-wave reversal is referred to as the First Floor Roof. Lindsay wrote that a five-wave reversal extending three months or more nearly always means that the formation is a Domed House.

The First Floor Roof is subsequently followed by another sharp rise, which is referred to as the Second Floor Wall. The Second Floor Wall is followed, and the entire 3PDh formation is capped, by a small head-and-shoulders pattern that resembles the cupola of a house. A horizontal line drawn through the left and right shoulder of the cupola suggests the roof of a second story. After the Cupola, a decline back to the beginning of the pattern begins, which normally will include at least one bounce (a final right shoulder) on the way down. Note that the First Floor Wall is balanced by the drop from the final right shoulder and the rise from the First Floor Roof is offset by the decline from the first right shoulder in the cupola. This gives the pattern a

square effect. At the same time, there is a **rounded effect at the top** due to the head-and-shoulders pattern.

Finally, the 3PDh formation can sometimes take the place not just of a single advance, but of a bear market. In other words, instead of going down, the market fluctuates back and forth and traces this familiar pattern. When it takes the place of a bear market, **the timing is irregular.** See examples of 3PDh formations with irregular timing in Table 3.1.

TABLE 3.1   *Three Peaks/Domed House*

Peak 1	Peak 2	Peak 3	Cupola
[1]10/18/1910	2/4/1911	6/191911	9/30/1912
10/22/1915	12/27/1915	3/16/1916	11/21/1916
[2]2/19/1918	5/15/1918	10/18/1918	11/3/1919
[2]6/5/1919	7/14/1919	8/12/1919	11/3/1919
[2]9/11/1922	10/14/1922	11/8/1922	3/20/1923
[2]2/5/1929	3/1/1929	5/4/1929	9/3/1929
[2]11/19/1935	3/6/1936	4/4/1936	3/10/1937
[2]7/10/1944	3/6/1945	5/29/1945	5/29/1946
[2]11/17/1945	12/10/1945	2/2/1946	5/29/1946
7/24/1947	10/20/1947	12/31/1947	6/15/1948
9/13/1951	1/22/1952	3/31/1952	1/5/1953
[2]7/6/1955	9/23/1955	4/6/1956	7/12/1957
4/6/1956	8/2/1956	12/31/1956	7/12/1957
8/3/1959	1/5/1960	6/9/1960	12/13/1961
11/18/1964	2/4/1965	5/14/1965	2/9/1966
5/5/1967	9/25/1967	1/8/1968	12/3/1968
	Domed House/Three Peaks		
Cupola	Peak 1	Peak 2	Peak 3
[1]6/17/1901	4/24/1902	9/19/1902	2/16/1903
[3]1/19/1906	10/9/1906	12/10/1906	1/7/1907

[1] *Off a bear market low*

[2] *Irregular count*

[3] *Off a bull market high*

Each of these segments of the 3PDh will be examined in detail in the chapters that follow. Before moving on, however, two simple concepts that Lindsay wrote about are reviewed.

Principle of Equalization

As the reader will soon discover, when we examine actual examples of the 3PDh pattern, real life doesn't always follow the "idealized" shape, time frame, or counts. Lindsay helps the analyst adjust for real-world uncertainties through the Principle of Equalization. Lindsay mentions the Principle of Equalization almost in passing. He defines it this way: *"When one formation falls short of the normal duration, the next one equalizes the total elapsed time by becoming longer."* Determining what a "normal" time frame is requires some detective work. He is very clear that the time between the three peaks is "normally" eight months, so we would expect to adjust the expected duration of the Domed House if the Three Peaks were longer or shorter than eight months. It was mentioned previously that Lindsay wrote that a five-wave reversal extending three months or more nearly always means that the formation is a Domed House. He didn't say whether there exists a minimum or maximum time period for the five-wave reversal (First Floor Roof), so a three-month estimate is all there is to work with. Adjusting the duration of the "count" (to determine the final top of the bull market) is not as simple as adding an extra month if the duration of the Three Peaks is a month short. Fortunately, it isn't complicated either and is explained in Chapter 5.

Domed House Before *Three Peaks*

There have been instances when the Domed House formation appeared before the Three Peaks formation. In this case, the Separating Line (explained in Chapter 4) follows the Domed House. *"Every time a clearly defined Domed House started at a **bear market** low, it was followed in due course by the Three Peaks before there was another major decline. There have been only a few cases when a major **bull** market high took the form of a Domed House followed by the Three Peaks. When the Three Peaks follows the Domed House, a complete retracement may not be made for a long time but it's always made."* This inversion of Lindsay's model is relatively rare and the reader would almost certainly notice it if it were to happen. Other than the formation that occurred in April 1938 to June 1940, the few examples given by Lindsay of this reversed pattern were all in the last decade of the 19th century and first decade of the 20th century. See Table 3.1 for examples.

Endnote

1. Unless otherwise indicated, all quotes in this chapter are taken from George Lindsay's self-published newsletter, *George Lindsay's Opinion*, during the years 1959–72.

Chapter 4

Three Peaks

"*The chief characteristic of this movement, as of the whole chart, is that the average makes rapid upside progress, but keeps going for only a short time. In between brief spurts, the average goes through long stretches of consolidation, or sideways movements.*"[1]
–George Lindsay

It is very easy to find the Three Peaks formation on a chart given the Separating Decline that follows. Once you understand the Three Peaks formation, you will begin seeing it everywhere. "*It is not unduly technical. All you have to do is fix a couple of shapes in your mind and then look at the charts with fresh eyes.*" At that point, the challenge will be to make certain that the Three Peaks pattern you have identified fulfills the requirements, or characteristics, of the 3PDh formation. This chapter introduces the reader to actual examples of the Three Peaks formation and prepares the reader for certain irregularities that have appeared in the past.

Characteristics and Irregularities

One can clearly see the three peaks toward the left side of Figure 4.1 followed by a sharp, three-wave sell-off. The Three Peaks pattern usually starts with a base (not shown), but Lindsay made clear that the base is not important in identifying the formation. From the bottom of the base, the average **rises sharply** to the First Peak. Lindsay wrote that, typically, the top of the peak has a rather flattened shape.

FIGURE 4.1   *Three Peaks.*

"The tops of all three peaks are usually in the same general price range. While there can be considerable variation in the exact levels, the symmetry of the whole formation is usually apparent." The "same general price range" is a relative statement and depends on the time frame you are examining. When looking **only** at a 3PDh formation, the Three Peaks may not appear to be in the "same general price range." But when the reader examines not just the 3PDh pattern but also the entire

advance that preceded the pattern, the phrase "same general price range" takes on a different meaning. After each peak is completed, prices react more than you would expect after such a short advance. Normally, the retracements after peaks one and two are of equal depth.

Lindsay's first example of a 3PDh formation starts at the bear market low in October 1946 (see Figure 4.2). Note that the period between Peaks One (February 8, 1947) and Three (October 10, 1947) is the standard eight months. In this example, Peak Two is above both Peak One and Peak Three.

An irregularity in the Three Peaks formation in 1947 is the decline from Peak One. The reaction after Peak One declined much more deeply than the decline after Peak Two. This irregularity is caused by the fractal nature of Peak One. This particular phenomenon is examined later in this chapter.

Figure 4.3 is an example Lindsay shared of the 3PDh formation at a bull market high. In this case, it was the February 1966 bull market high. Note that the advance into Peak Three on May 14, 1965, was preceded by a short consolidation during most of February and March just as the advance into Peak One was preceded by a short consolidation from late September to early November. *"Whenever the market spends so much time moving sideways, we look for indications of a Three Peaks-Domed House pattern."* Lindsay made note of the fact that the time between Peak One and Peak Three in this case was six months—the minimum duration. *"In a major formation, the typical duration from the top of the First Peak to the high of the Third is about eight months. It has never been less than six nor more*

52 *George Lindsay and the Art of Technical Analysis*

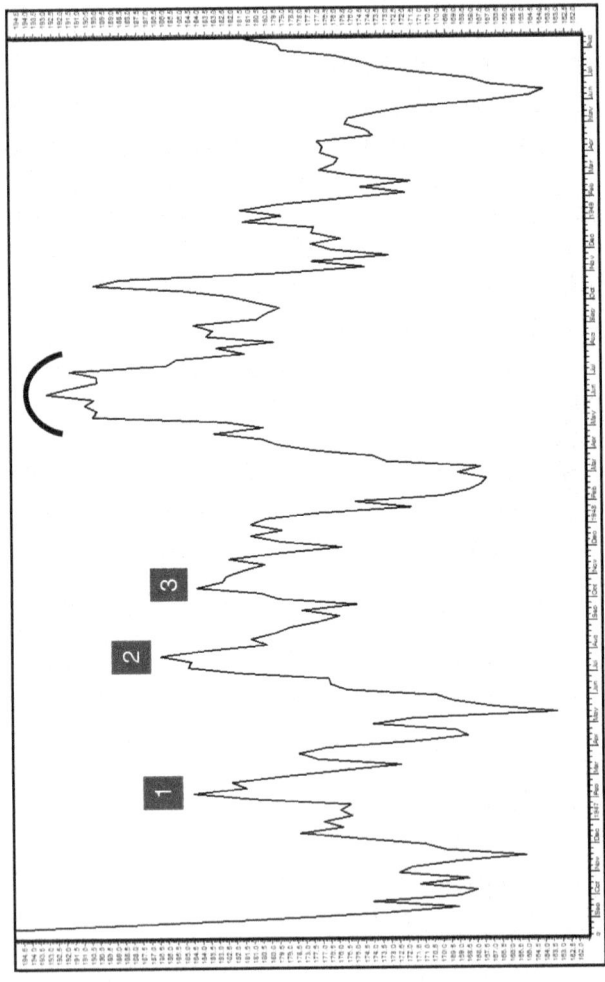

FIGURE 4.2 Three Peaks (1946–48). *Chart created by MetaStock®.*

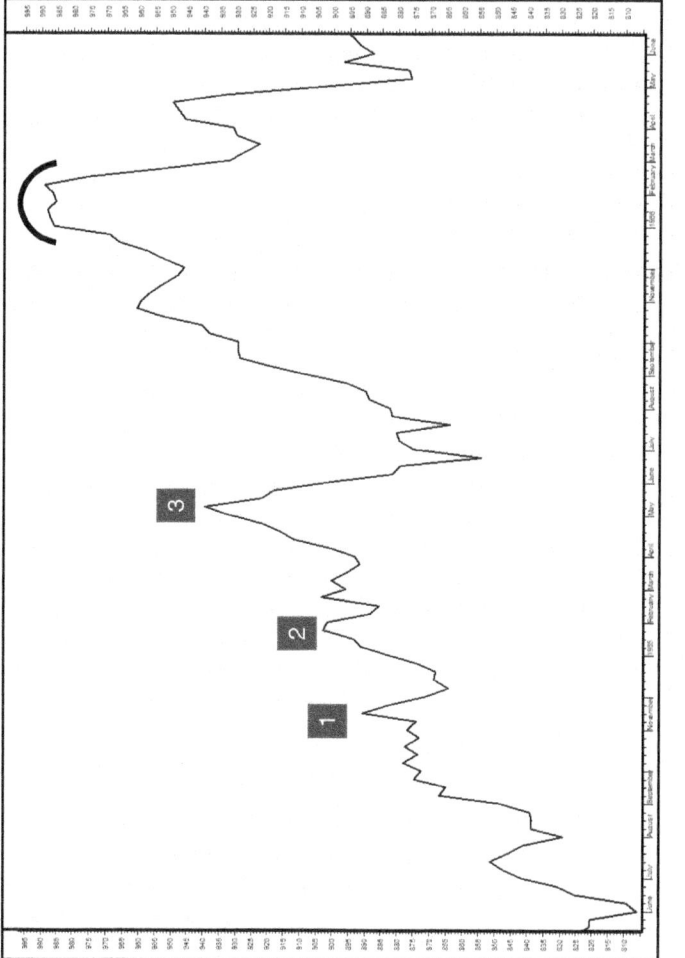

FIGURE 4.3 Three Peaks (1964–66). Chart created by MetaStock®.

than ten, and usually has varied between seven and eight." He also noted that the time period between the start of the consolidation in late September (prior to Peak One) and Peak Three was eight months—the normal duration. He doesn't explain this; he simply makes note of it. But it is one of many examples of how counts can differ and the analyst must show flexibility, even some imagination, when working with this geometric formation. One particular example of flexibility: If the time between Peak One and Peak Three is short (less than six months), look to see whether Peak Three has the "flattened shape" (rounded top) discussed previously. If a trading range forms after the highest day (the peak) of this rounded top at Peak Three, and there is a point at the end of the trading range where price falls off suddenly, then measuring from Peak One to that point usually causes the time span between Peaks One and Three to meet the minimum required time—six months. Variation in counts is dealt with more in Chapter 3, "The Phenomenon."

Fractals

Sometimes a 3PDh formation will occur within a single peak of a larger ("major") formation. Lindsay referred to a 3PDh pattern inside of a single Peak as a "minor" formation. Modern readers will know this manifestation as a fractal. Figure 4.4 breaks out the fractal structure that created Peak One of the 1946–48 3PDh formation. The horizontal line helps delineate the fact that the Separating Decline after the fractal's Third Peak extended below either of the reactions from Peaks One or Two as is required for the 3PDh formation.

Three Peaks 55

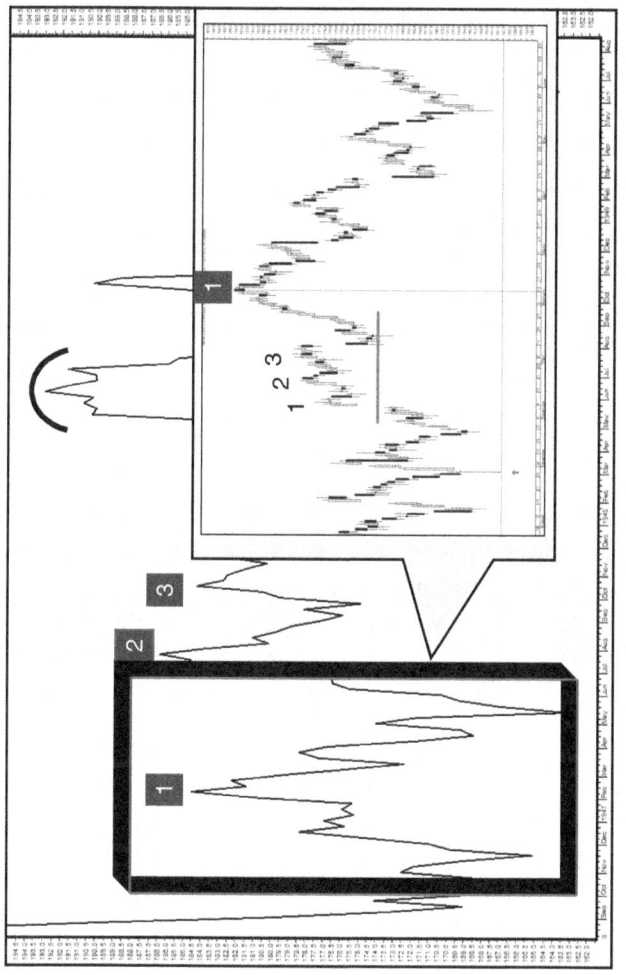

FIGURE 4.4 Three Peaks (1946–48). Chart created by MetaStock®.

Separating Declines are covered in the next section. One can just make out the head-and-shoulders top that forms the Cupola, but a five-wave reversal that creates a First Floor Roof is definitely missing. After the Cupola, the index returns to the beginning (bottom) of the formation as is expected of any 3PDh pattern.

"*Any one of the Three Peaks (in a major formation) can double as the Domed House of a minor formation. As a rule, it is more likely to be the Third Peak, rather than the first one, as in this case.*"

Recognizing possible fractals is crucial to trading the 3PDh model. A relatively severe decline has always followed a Three Peak/Domed House pattern even when the pattern is contained within another pattern. A severe decline is expected after Peak Three of a 3PDh pattern as well. If the 3PDh pattern is a fractal, a relatively severe decline can be expected here too. A 3PDh pattern inside of one of the peaks is a warning that a big decline may be coming because it will need to undercut one of the previous reactions from a peak. By being aware of fractals, one can avoid big declines or even profit from them.

Separating Decline

After the Third Peak, a rather severe downtrend begins. It is called the Separating Decline because it separates the Three Peaks from the Domed House formation that follows (see Figure 4.5). The Separating Decline is a three-wave decline usually composed of at least two declining waves. The bottom of the second declining wave is always at a lower level than at least one of the reactions from Peaks One or Two, and often it is lower than both. Unless **at least** one of the two reaction lows is breached, the formation under consideration does not qualify as a Separating Decline and, by extension, the previous formation is simply three random peaks and not a Three Peaks pattern. One should have no trouble identifying the Separating Declines in Figures 4.2 and 4.3. They are the declines that immediately follow the Third Peak in each chart. Note that in Figure 4.2, the Separating Decline only breaches the reaction low following Peak Two and not Peak One (due to the fractal causing an abnormally deep decline after Peak One), whereas the Separating Decline in Figure 4.3 breaches both reaction lows following both Peaks One and Two.

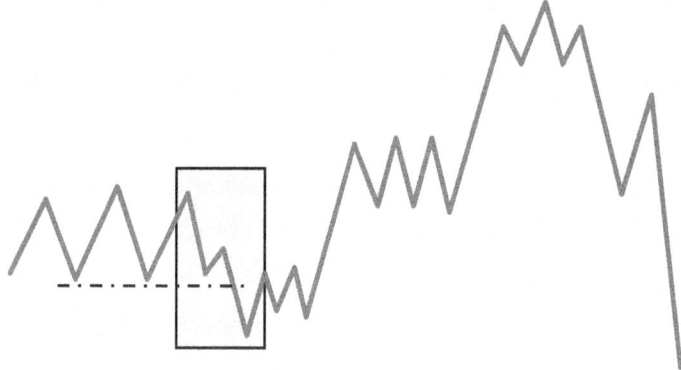

FIGURE 4.5 *Separating Decline.*

Important Note: Toward the end of an advance that has proceeded for a year or longer with a subnormal rate of gain, the convention that the Separating Decline must dip under the low of a previous sell-off is not required. This exception is explored in Chapter 6, "The Tri-Day Method."

Conclusion

The Separating Decline dropping below a reaction from a previous peak makes it appear as if the advance is getting tired. One can imagine traders and investors exiting the market in expectation of an extended decline. Perhaps it can be interpreted as a bearish head-and-shoulders top. The market participant who is aware of the 3PDh model is unlikely to be fooled by a failed head-and-shoulders top. Even a casual market participant acquainted with the 3PDh model will not only recognize a fractal within a peak being formed and suspect that a 3PDh is under construction, but also be prepared to avoid, or profit from, the coming downturn within the peak being observed, understand that a time is coming to reenter the trade, continue tracking the formation of a possible Three Peaks pattern, again avoid (or profit from) the approaching Separating Decline, and, finally, be mentally prepared to reenter the trade for what is possibly the biggest move of the bull market. All this while other traders and investors have become worn out from what they perceive as unprecedented volatility. Chapter 5, "A Domed House," examines the Domed House pattern and its individual building blocks.

Endnote

1. Unless otherwise indicated, all quotes in this chapter are taken from George Lindsay's self-published newsletter, *George Lindsay's Opinion*, during the years 1959–72.

Chapter 5

A Domed House

"The most typical Three Peak-Domed House formations start at a bear market low. When this has been true, the highest point in the pattern has never equaled the top of the previous major bull market. Not all of the minor bull markets of the past have taken the shape of the Three Peaks and Domed House, but most of them have."[1] *–George Lindsay*

After the Separating Decline, the Domed House formation begins (see Figure 5.1). Like the Three Peaks pattern, the Domed House pattern is *"distinguished by advances and declines which travel many points in a straight line. But the movements never last very long. In between the few explosive moves, the market spends much of the time backing and filling in a comparatively narrow range."* By keeping this simple requirement of both patterns in mind at all times, the analyst will avoid the mistake of seeing 3PDh formations everywhere and the losses associated with false attribution of the pattern. This chapter breaks down the Domed House formation into its component parts, identifies and discusses the characteristics of each component part, and lays out the counts and counting methods necessary to identify and confirm the formation.

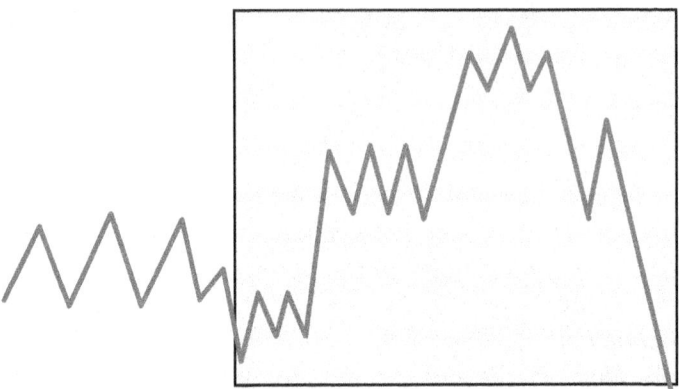

FIGURE 5.1   *Domed House.*

Bases

The Domed House begins with some kind of base. It is important to distinguish whether the base is irregular or symmetrical. To be a satisfactory base, whether irregular or symmetrical, there should be a rebound from the low of the Separating Decline and then two secondary dips after the rebound from the low. Lindsay makes it clear that one dip doesn't suffice; there must be two dips. Determining the number of dips, however, is somewhat arbitrary, as one can see in the examples that follow.

Determining the nature of the base (irregular or symmetrical) was critical to Lindsay because the labeling of the base will determine the origin date of the count. Also critical to Lindsay was the determination of whether the base was longer or shorter than "normal." Unfortunately, Lindsay never revealed what time period he considered to be normal. It does appear, from the examples he gave, that a base lasting one month is shorter than "normal" and a base lasting approximately two months is to be considered "normal." The count (221–224 calendar days) is used to estimate the final day of the bull market—usually to within three days. Counting 221–224 days forward from the determined point of origin will direct one to either the exact date of a bull market top or an easily recognized and defined point near the bull market top. The uncanny ability of the model to pinpoint the end of a bull market to within such a small time frame is what makes the 3PDh model so amazing and Lindsay's genius so obvious.

Lindsay never actually **defines** a Symmetrical Base, opting instead to **identify** bases in his charts as symmetric or irregular. The base in the idealized chart example (see Figure 5.2) is an example of a Symmetrical Base. When a Symmetrical Base is present, we begin our count from the bottom of the second dip following the Separating Decline, as shown in Figure 5.2.

If the secondary sell-off (the final sell-off in the base) is too shallow (an ascending base) to call the base symmetrical, we cannot count from it. The span must be counted from the low of the base, that is, the bottom of Separating Decline. Even if an ascending base is symmetrical, the count must originate before the secondary sell-off.

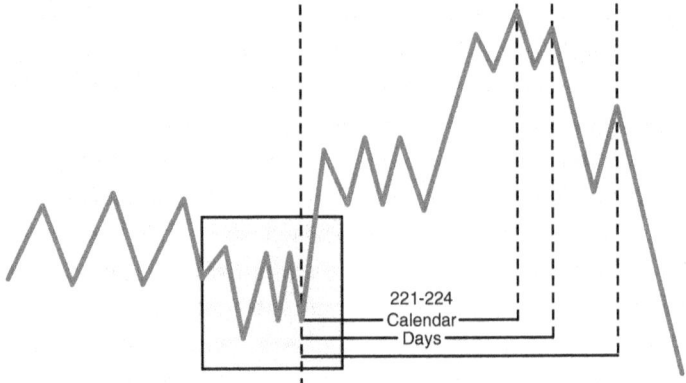

FIGURE 5.2 *Base—Symmetrical.*

Figure 5.3, which shows the Domed House in 1938, contains an example of a Symmetrical Base as identified by Lindsay. Note how the base is descending but contained within two parallel lines, giving it a symmetric presence.

Counts

The typical duration from the **end** of a base (bottom of the First Floor Wall) to the peak of a Domed House is 221–224 calendar days (seven months plus eight to ten calendar days, or 32 weeks). Note that counts are made using calendar days, not trading days. While exceptions can be found to all of Lindsay's "rules," it is his rules concerning the counts that seem to have the most exceptions and to be the most arbitrary. For every rule Lindsay listed, an exception can be found such that one has to wonder how Lindsay decided which example was

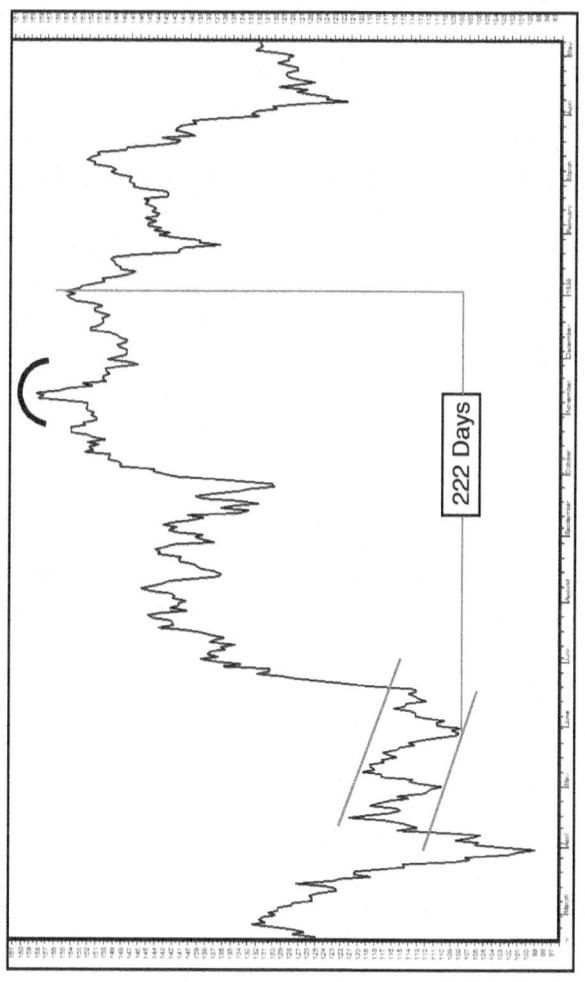

FIGURE 5.3 Symmetrical Base. Chart created by MetaStock®.

to become his "rule"! The rules that follow should be thought of more as rules of thumb, heuristics, at best. Lindsay even lists several examples that called market tops in the 20th century, none of which met his requirements for counts. They are included in Chapter 3, "The Phenomenon," in Table 3.1. *"Movements of very irregular duration have occurred in the course of Three Peak-Domed House patterns. We then go by the shape of the chart, and not by the number of days."* Part III of this book describes the Lindsay Timing Model, which Lindsay holds out as a way to make sense of all the seeming contradictions that follow. Bypassing the following heuristics would be a mistake for the reader, however, as one must not only be acquainted with them, but be actively looking for each of these possibilities in order to ascertain which count is correctly confirmed by the Lindsay Timing Model. As Lindsay wrote, *"The market is never exactly the same twice. To have a chance of applying any theory satisfactorily, a student must be familiar with all past examples of each formation, so that the variations in each recurrence will not confuse him."*

Domed House Longer Than Normal

Lindsay gave only one example of a longer-than-normal Domed House (see Figure 5.4). This was a formation in which the Cupola formed in December 1968. From the bottom of the base to the top of the Cupola, 255 days passed. He gives two explanations for its extended period.

A Domed House 65

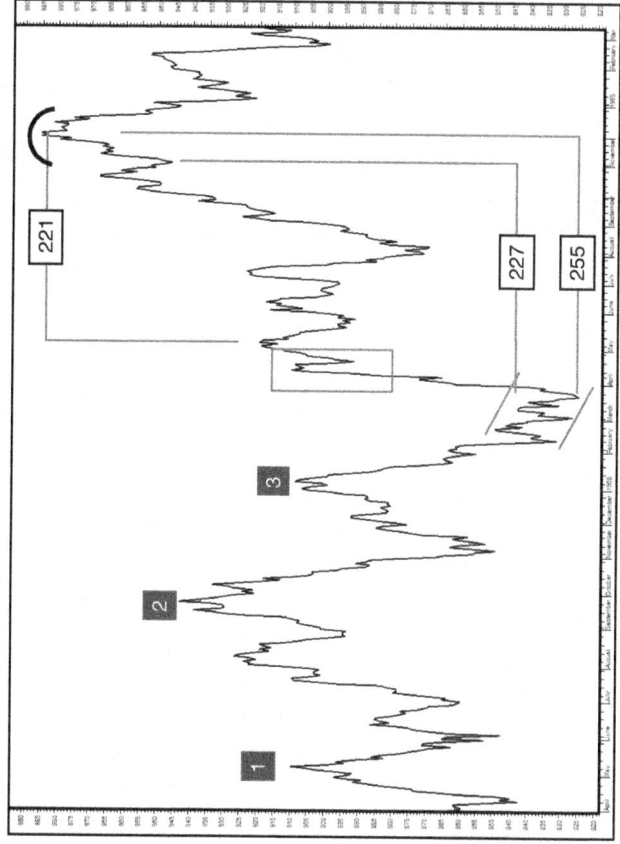

FIGURE 5.4 Long Domed House. Chart created by MetaStock®.

1. A Descending Base Instead of a Normal Ascending Base

Lindsay's first explanation for a Domed House that was longer than the normal 221–224 calendar days was that the base was of the descending variety. The reader will notice that the base in Figure 5.3 was **also** a descending base but the Domed House was **shorter** than normal, and certainly shorter than the Domed House in Figure 5.4. Lindsay doesn't address that apparent contradiction, but we will note that the formation in Figure 5.3 was a reversed pattern, a Domed House followed by Three Peaks.

2. The Base Was Shorter Than Normal

Lindsay wrote that the base being shorter than normal explained the longer-than-normal Domed House based on the "principle of equalization." The base measured 37 days. *"Under the principle of equalization, this meant that the next move would probably be longer than normal."*

It is worth highlighting that a count of 227 days from the bottom of the First Floor Wall precisely targets the absolute bottom of the left shoulder of the Cupola. It is also of interest that a count of 221 days forward, from the top of the First Floor Roof (the beginning of the five-wave reversal), targets a date (December 10th) in the heart of the topping formation (looking for the "center of gravity" in a top formation is a favorite technique of Lindsay's, and this approach is dealt with, in depth, in Part III, "The Lindsay Timing Model"). The preceding counts are examples of an easily recognized and defined point near the bull market top.

Domed House Shorter Than Normal

Lindsay also addressed the situation of a Domed House being shorter than normal. He listed two irregularities that the reader should be aware of.

1. Missing First Floor Roof

If a Domed House is **shorter than normal,** the count will usually end at the peak of either of the two right shoulders following the absolute top. In 1947, the base was symmetrical (see Figure 5.5) yet the count extended to the right shoulder in 1948. Lindsay notes that an analyst should have suspected a shorter-than-normal Domed House, prior to its completion, because where a five-wave reversal was expected, price simply slid off for seven days. Lindsay, however, failed to explain how an analyst could know where or when a five-wave reversal should be expected! The time required to build the First Floor Wall varies considerably between formations. In hindsight, the absence of a First Floor Roof (five-wave reversal) told us that the Domed House would be shorter than normal. *"The failure of the 5 reversals to appear implied that this would be an unusually short-lived domed house."*

2. Patterns at Secular Bull Market Tops

This chapter's opening quote from Lindsay, *"The most typical Three Peak-Domed House formations start at a bear market low,"* does not mean to imply that most 3PDh formations start at bear market lows. Rather, the intent was to bring attention to the fact that 3PDh patterns that begin at bear market lows normally adhere to Lindsay's rules more faithfully. Contrast those

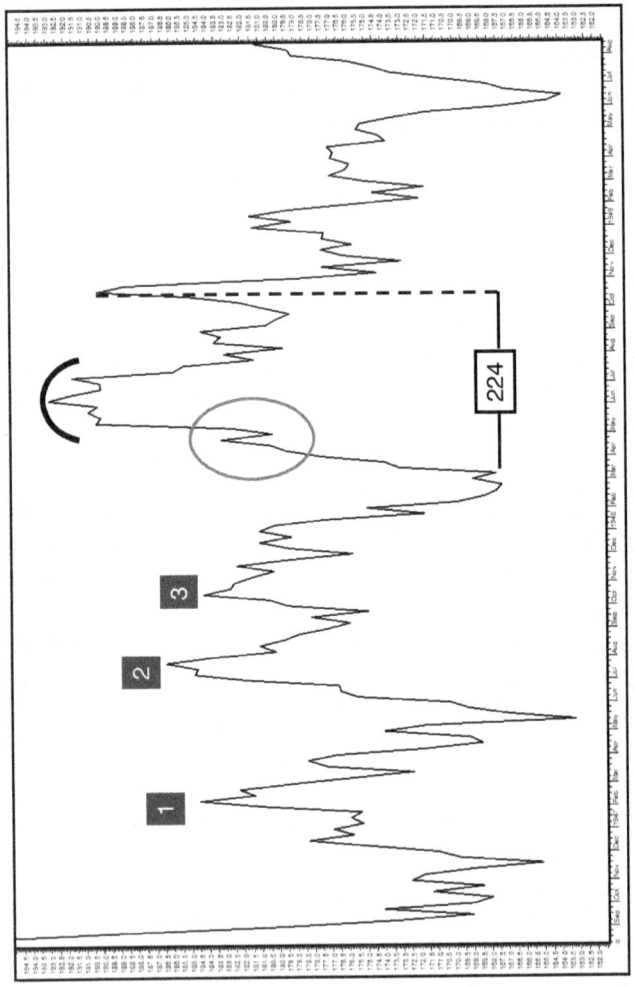

FIGURE 5.5 Short Domed House. Chart created by MetaStock®.

patterns with the patterns that appear at the end of secular bull markets. *"The patterns which start in the latter part of a major bull market do not normally last as long as those that begin at a bear market low, and they are often less symmetrical."*

Since a Domed House at the top of a bull market seldom lasts as long as the formation that begins at a bear market low, we count the span to the peak of the Dome from the bottom of the Separating Decline or from an even earlier low such as the bottom of the sell-off from the Second Peak and sometimes even the First Peak sell-off.

Again, the preceding "rules" are more "rules-of-thumb" than hard-and-fast rules. The Lindsay Timing Model explained in Part IV, "The Counts," gives the analyst the confirming information and confidence needed to sort out and determine which of the possible counts is the correct one. *"Variations of this sort must always be expected. They are hard to predict, but a technician familiar with the underlying principles should have no trouble recognizing them when they occur."*

First Floor Wall

Once the base following the Separating Decline is completed by the second dip, or test of the bottom, price is then expected to shoot up in a fast, short-lived advance. This is called the First Floor Wall of the Domed House (see Figure 5.6). The advance from the bottom to the top of the First Floor Wall should be extremely powerful—almost straight up. A wall that appears to be broken into two advancing waves by an intervening wave may contain no roof and be rushing to its completion at the Cupola. This implies that the Domed House will be shorter than normal. Again, Lindsay did not share how to determine whether the roof is missing prior to completion of the pattern. While a missing roof may be known with certainty only in hindsight, the chance that a roof may be missing is an important possibility of which to be aware.

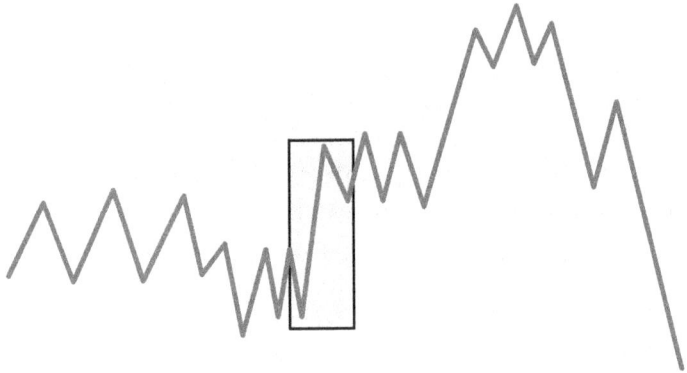

FIGURE 5.6 *First Floor Wall.*

First Floor Roof

This First Floor Wall is followed by a five-wave reversal pattern that serves to consolidate the sharp rise. The five-wave reversal is referred to as the First Floor Roof (see Figure 5.7). Lindsay wrote that a five-wave reversal extending three months or more nearly always means that the formation is a Domed House. To help identify the five reversals, look for a period in which the average makes no net progress over a **significant period of time**. The First Floor Roof is similar to a triangle in that it usually has five reversals. After the fifth reversal is completed, the main uptrend is resumed.

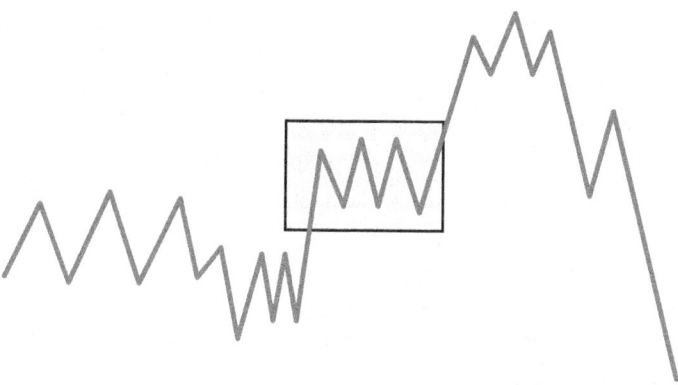

FIGURE 5.7   *First Floor Roof.*

Characteristics

The First Floor Roof is not as straightforward as the First Floor Wall. The reader will find it helpful to be aware of both the characteristics of the Roof as well as the anomalies that have been known to occur.

Roof Rallies

Lindsay wrote, *"Usually, both of the rallies within a triangle are of about the same amplitude."* This characteristic can be a big help in identifying the First Floor Roof of a 3PDh formation, particularly when the First Floor

Roof is not of the shape expected. Once the roof is identified, the rest of the suspected formation is easily confirmed or invalidated. Figure 5.8 breaks out the First Floor Roof from the 1968 top formation. Note that the first decline is a false start (to be discussed later). Once the high of the First Floor Wall is complete, however, wave 1 of the roof begins its decline in earnest. Waves 2 and 4 are of equal length in distance covered (price, not time). Another interesting aspect of this particular roof is the deep drop made during wave 5. At the time, a decline of this magnitude would have been fairly disconcerting to the analyst. But the knowledge that (the assumed) waves 2 and 4 were equal should have given him or her confidence to stay with the inferred pattern. Other than the wave-5 plunge, the 1968 First Floor Roof stays true to the idealized formation in its horizontal character.

Despite the horizontal roof depicted in Figure 5.8 and Lindsay's idealized chart, it appears that an equal number of roofs tend to decline as in Figure 5.3. Having noted this, the analyst still needs to be alert for variations.

Anomalies

The following two anomalies, while not common, have occurred enough times that the reader will find it advantageous to be prepared to see them again in the future.

Missing Roof

It is extremely rare, but sometimes it does happen that the roof is composed of a simple pullback, or short

A Domed House 73

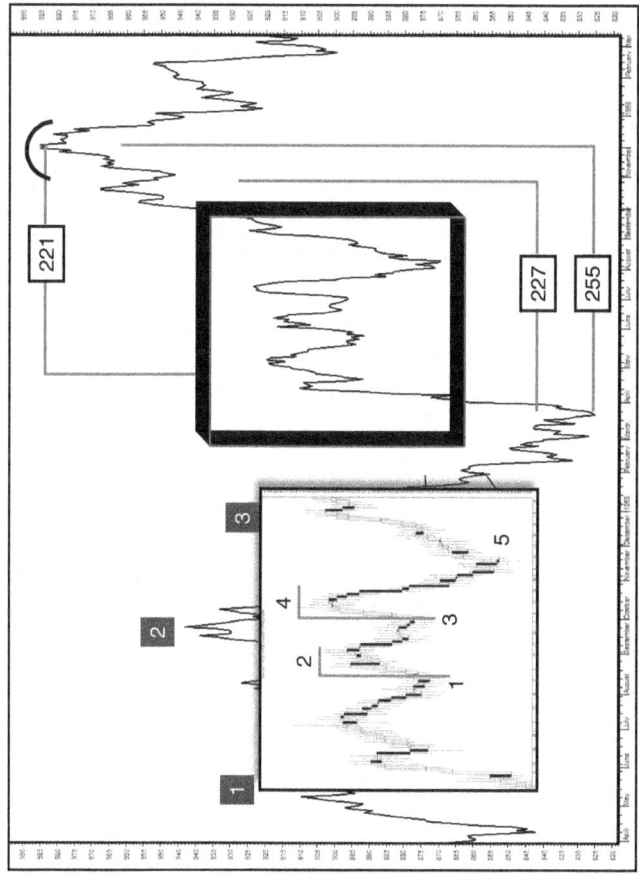

FIGURE 5.8 Roof Rallies. *Chart created by MetaStock®.*

reaction, rather than the five reversals we would normally expect.

As discussed previously, if this happens, the missing roof implies that the Domed House will be unusually short-lived. An example of this phenomenon can be seen in the 1948 formation in Figure 5.5.

False Starts

Sometimes what is perceived as the top of the First Floor Wall is not correct. Oftentimes we see a little dip after the strong advance of the wall and it is tempting to count that as the first reversal of the roof. *"This is a peculiarity which comes up in many triangles and similar chart patterns, both in the average and individual stocks. If the first sell-off in a trading range is shallower than the next two, it may not count as the First Reversal at all, even though it lines up with them symmetrically on the chart."* Figures 5.3 and 5.4 both show false starts to the ensuing triangles. This irregularity should not provide anything more than an annoyance to the analyst. Being aware of the possibility of this peccadillo will help to avoid unnecessary frustration.

Second Floor Wall

The First Floor Roof is subsequently followed by another sharp rise, referred to as the Second Floor Wall (see Figure 5.9). The Second Floor Wall, like the First Floor Wall, is characterized by an abrupt spurt upward. Lindsay also said to watch for high volume during the "construction" of the wall because that too is a characteristic of the wall.

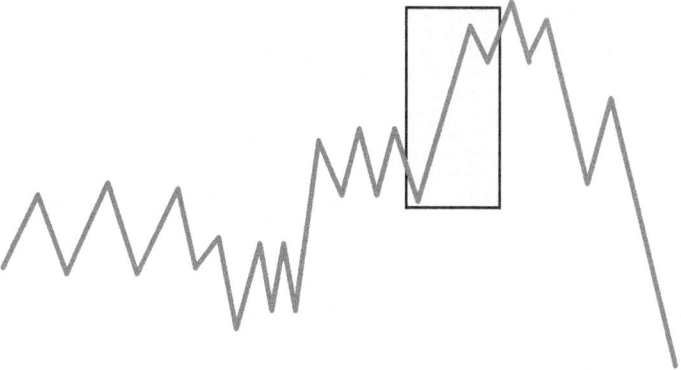

FIGURE 5.9   *Second Floor Wall.*

The Cupola and the Decline

Once the advance from the First Floor Roof (the Second Floor Wall) is complete, the average pulls back slightly. Price can then be expected to make a run to yet another new high. *"Normally, the average gains less on the last leg of a major advance (despite continued high volume) than on most of the previous legs. If this is not true, the market is not making a top."* In other words, the advance slows down as it gets older. The new high is not held and the average quickly pulls back again, retracing the entire gain. Once the new and final high has been passed and prices start to drop, they usually do not drop very far before they start to rally again and form a clear-cut right shoulder or the right side of the second-story rooftop (see Figure 5.10). A horizontal line drawn through the left and right shoulder of the Cupola suggests the roof of a second story. These movements suggest a cupola or a small dome on the top of a building, hence the formation is called a Domed House. The entire 3PDh formation is capped by a small head-and-shoulders pattern that resembles the cupola of a house.

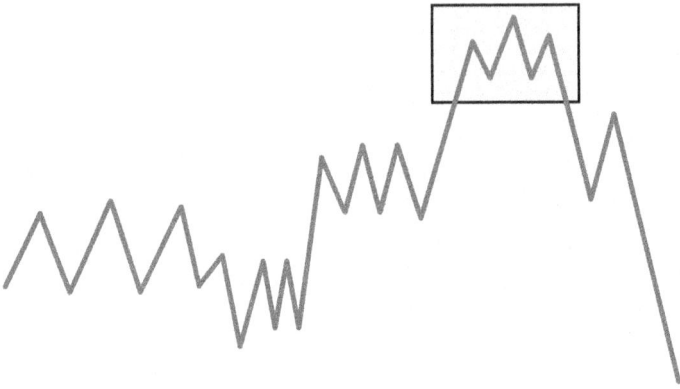

FIGURE 5.10   *Cupola.*

An abrupt decline then follows that right shoulder. This larger decline from the right shoulder of the Cupola precedes another short recovery. The top of this second recovery often ends at a level, relative to the First Story Roof, which suggests that it is the right side of the First Story Roof. This advance can also be interpreted as the right shoulder of a different, larger head-and-shoulders formation. In this head-and-shoulders formation, the triangle-shaped First Floor Roof functions as the left shoulder. *"Note that the First Floor Wall is balanced by the drop from the final right shoulder, and the rise from the First Floor Roof is offset by the decline from the first right shoulder in the Cupola. This gives the pattern a square effect. At the same time there is a rounded effect at the top due to the head-and-shoulders pattern."*

After this second, lower-right shoulder is completed, the average drops back to the ultimate low of the base where the Domed House began. *"But there has never been an exception to the rule that the entire gain in a Domed House has eventually been cancelled."* The knowledge that the entire gain of the previous (approximately) two-plus years will be wiped out is what makes familiarity with the 3PDh formation so empowering and potentially profitable. Even if a trader misses the top of the Cupola, he or she still has plenty of time to profit from shorting the market, given the size of the move ahead. The size of that move is easily ascertained by measuring the remaining distance to the bottom of the 3PDh formation.

Conclusion

In a newsletter dated September 4, 1968, Lindsay shared some tips for recognizing a Domed House that the reader should find helpful: *"Here's how the advance of January 1967 could have been recognized as a Domed House. All technical measurements of the market were terrifically strong; the advance-decline line, odd-lot indexes, volume and momentum studies, etc. They were entirely too favorable for the move to be just a rally in a bear market. On the contrary, they suggested a major bull market had begun. Yet after rising only three weeks, the Dow-Jones Industrials stalled. In a genuine bull market and after such a powerful start, the average would have kept going. It wouldn't have hesitated as long as it did before and after [the top of the First Floor Wall]. It was a combination of a bullish technical position and a sideways movement which began prematurely and lasted unduly long. The only way of reconciling the contradictions was to assume that a Domed House was under way."* In his August 16, 1972, newsletter, Lindsay wrote that the most important long-term interval lasts about 15 years or somewhat longer. *"It is needed to understand the Domed House fully."* The 15-year interval is covered in Part IV.

George Lindsay is most well known for his Three Peaks and a Domed House model, no doubt due to its descriptive, if awkward, name. While many technical analysts are familiar with the name of the model, very few have any experience using it. Even a superficial familiarity with the model should be of great benefit to the most passive investor. While the array of possible counts may seem confusing at first, Lindsay shared several examples (see Table 3.1) in which only the basic form of the model was present at several market tops and the counts that he had established were missing. The 3PDh model is one of those few methods that will yield results to the beginner and continue yielding as more effort is expended on the part of the student. Part III examines the Lindsay Timing Model, which is both its own, free-standing model as well as the concluding technique for determining the correct count for the 3PDh model.

Endnote

1. Unless otherwise indicated, all quotes in this chapter are taken from George Lindsay's self-published newsletter, *George Lindsay's Opinion,* during the years 1959–72.

Chapter 6

The Tri-Day Method

"It is called the Tri-Day Method because you need to know the price of the stock average on just three days in order to compute the level of the final bottom. The calculation can be made shortly after the bull market high."[1] –George Lindsay

Lindsay explained his Tri-Day Method (see Figure 6.1) in a series of five supplements to his newsletter from May to September 1959. In them he described a new method of calculating the level of bear market lows using the Three Peaks and a Domed House formation.

The name "Tri-Day Method" comes from the fact that to forecast the price level of a bottom, what is needed is the level of the average at just three points:

- Point F (the top of Peak Three)
- Point G (the bottom of the Separating Decline)
- Point N (the top of the Domed House)

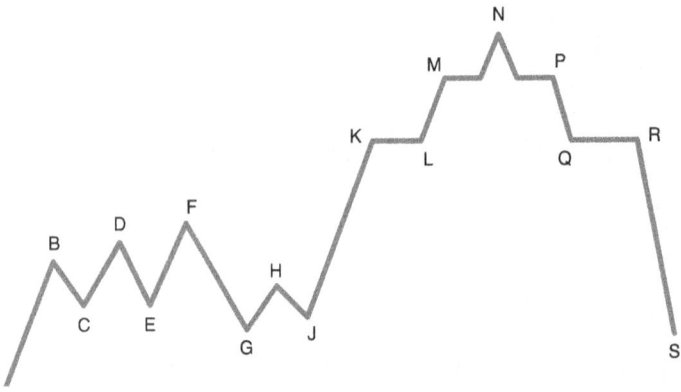

FIGURE 6.1 *Tri-Day Method.*

From these three points, two values are needed to get started:

- (F–G): The extent of the loss from Peak Three to the bottom of the Separating Decline.
- (N–G): The extent of the gain from the bottom of the Separating Decline to the top of the Domed House.

Swingover Ratio

The ratio (N–G)/(F–G) is calculated and referred to as the "Swingover ratio" (S.O.). This Swingover ratio is used as a multiplier. When the Swingover is less than 2, the exact Swingover becomes the multiplier. When the Swingover is 2 or greater, the multiplier is simply 2. The multiplier cannot exceed 2 except in one circumstance: If the **highest point** in the whole Three Peaks formation (it does not matter which peak is highest) is ten months or longer from the top of the Domed House (point N), then 2.2 becomes the upper limit on the multiplier instead of the customary 2.

Calculation Steps

The target price of the final bottom is calculated using simple math. The steps presented here illustrate the process of determining the targeted bottom:

1. Determine the length of the Separating Decline (F–G).
2. Determine the length of the rally from the bottom of the Separating Decline to the top of the Domed House (N–G).
3. Determine the ratio between steps one and two (the Swingover, S.O.).
   A. If it is less than 2, the ratio is the multiplier.
   B. If it is equal to or greater than 2, then 2 is the multiplier.
   C. If the time between the highest peak and the top of the Domed House is 10 months or longer, 2.2 becomes the upper limit of the multiplier.
4. [(N–G) × S.O.] – (F–G) = the number of points that can be expected to be lost following the top of the market at Point N.

Lindsay wrote that either intraday or closing prices can be used for these calculations.

The 3PDh of 1915–16 provides an excellent, clear example of the Tri-Day Method (see Figure 6.2). Peak Three, or Point F, in the Dow was at 96.08 on March 16, 1916. The Separating Decline took it down to 84.96 at Point G on April 22nd for a loss of 11.12 points (F–G).

During the rise from Point G to Point N at 110.15, the Dow gained 25.19 points. Dividing 25.19 by 11.12 results in a Swingover of 2.26. Given that the highest point in the Three Peaks formation (Peak One on December 27, 1915) was more than 10 months from Point N, the upper limit on the multiplier becomes 2.2. The Swingover of 2.26 is limited to 2.2.

Multiply 25.19 (N–G) by 2.2. The product is 55.42. Subtract 11.12 (F–G) from 55.42 and the difference is 44.30. This is the number of points the Dow will be expected to lose between points N and S.

Subtract 44.30 from 110.15 (N) and the remainder is 65.85. This is the price target of the Tri-Day Method and should be a low of major importance. The actual bear market low on December 19, 1917, was 65.95.

The Tri-Day Method 83

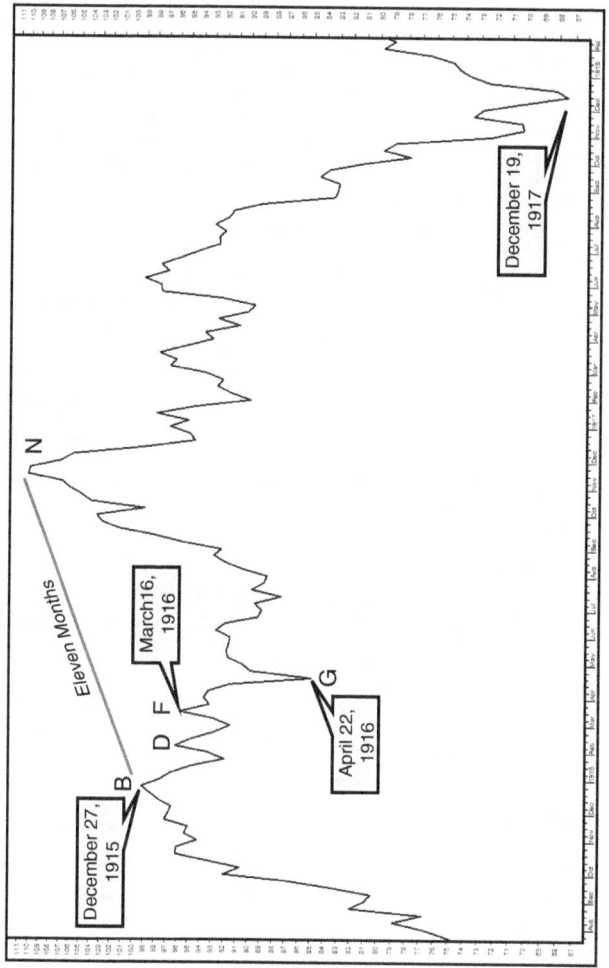

FIGURE 6.2 *Tri-Day Method. Chart created by MetaStock®.*

Model 3

Lindsay allowed for three variations, or models, of the 3PDh formation. In Model 1, the three peaks are a series of ascending highs, with Peak Three as the highest. This is the Three Peaks example in Figure 6.1. In Model 2, Peak Three is the lowest peak. In Model 3, the decline from Point D (Peak Two) to Point E is a three-wave affair with an upward reaction, or wave 2, separating two declining waves. The low at Point E lies below the first low at Point C, fulfilling the 3PDh requirement of a reaction to a low below a previous reaction low. From there, prices advance to Point F, which is the highest point of the entire formation. The reaction to Point G holds above the level of E. This is the only model in which the reaction from Point F does not undercut one of the previous two reactions. When the First Floor Wall is retraced almost all the way back to the bottom of the Separating Decline, a Model 3 can be assumed. In Model 3, the downtrend that ordinarily runs from H to J becomes the Separating Decline. In the case of a Model 3 Three Peaks formation, we count from this higher bottom to the top of the Domed House to determine the Swingover (as opposed to counting from the reaction low, which undercut a previous low).

The 3PDh formation of 1951–52 (see Figure 6.3) provides an example of Model 3 when the average dropped from 280.29 at F in August 1952 to 263.06 at G in October, a loss of 17.23 points.

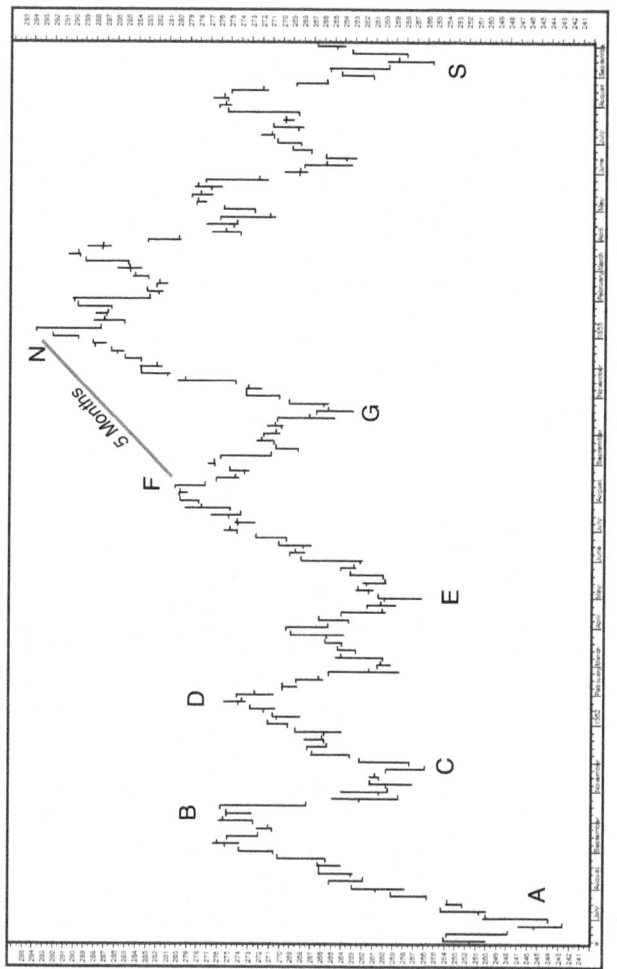

FIGURE 6.3 Tri-Day Method—Model 3. Chart created by *MetaStock®*.

The Dow then rose to 293.79 at N on January 5th, a gain of 30.73 points. Divide 30.73 by 17.23. The dividend is 1.78. That's the Swingover. Since it is less than the upper limit of 2 on the multiplier, the exact Swingover becomes the multiplier.

Multiply 30.73, the gain from G to N, by 1.78. The product is 54.70. From that amount, subtract 17.23, the loss from F to G. The remainder is 37.47. This is the number of points the Dow should lose between N and S.

Deduct 37.47 from 293.79, the price at N. The remainder of 256.32 is the calculated Tri-Day price at S. The actual low of September 13, 1953, was 255.49.

Note that the intraday low at E exceeded the low at C by 0.30 points. Also note that the count was not from this low but from a higher low at G.

Complex Arrangement

Unlike the previous examples, there are times when a more complicated method must be used. A Complex Arrangement occurs when an additional 3PDh is found contained in the First Floor Roof. This situation is often preceded by prices rising gradually in the early stages of an advance. From 1926 to the middle of 1928, from December 1917 to February 1919, and from 1943 to mid-1945, the pattern was the same. The Dow crept up steadily, but the rate of gain was much less than is normal in bull markets. Similar to the Model 3 scenario, the reaction to Point G holds above the level of E.

Toward the end of an advance that has proceeded for a year or longer with a subnormal rate of gain, the convention that one of the declines must dip under the low of a previous sell-off is not required.

Whenever a Domed House is complex, the Swingover multiplier must be computed with reference to the Three Peaks contained within the First Floor Roof, the formation nearest to the final top.

The entire movement between the low in June 1928 and the high of 1929 is a Complex Domed House, an initial Three Peaks formation followed by a second 3PDh formation contained within the First Floor Roof (see Figure 6.4). The Dow made a high of 327.08 on May 4, 1929. It dropped to 293.42 on May 27th. This was the Separating Decline of the formation in the First Floor Roof. The loss was 33.66 points.

The Dow then rose to 381.17 on September 3rd, a gain of 87.75 points. Divide 87.75 by 33.66. The ratio is 2.61. That's the Swingover. Less than 10 months passed between the highest point of the 3PDh formation (May 4, 1929) and Point N the following September, so the upper limit on the multiplier is 2.

In 1928, the Dow was at 220.96 at Point F on June 2nd. It dropped to 201.96 on June 18th, a loss of 19 points. This was the Separating Decline of the Three Peaks pattern that preceded the entire Domed House.

From 201.96 at G on June 18th, the Dow rose to 381.17 at Point N on September 3, 1929, a gain of 179.21 points in the Domed House. Multiply 179.21 by 2. The product is 358.42.

88   George Lindsay and the Art of Technical Analysis

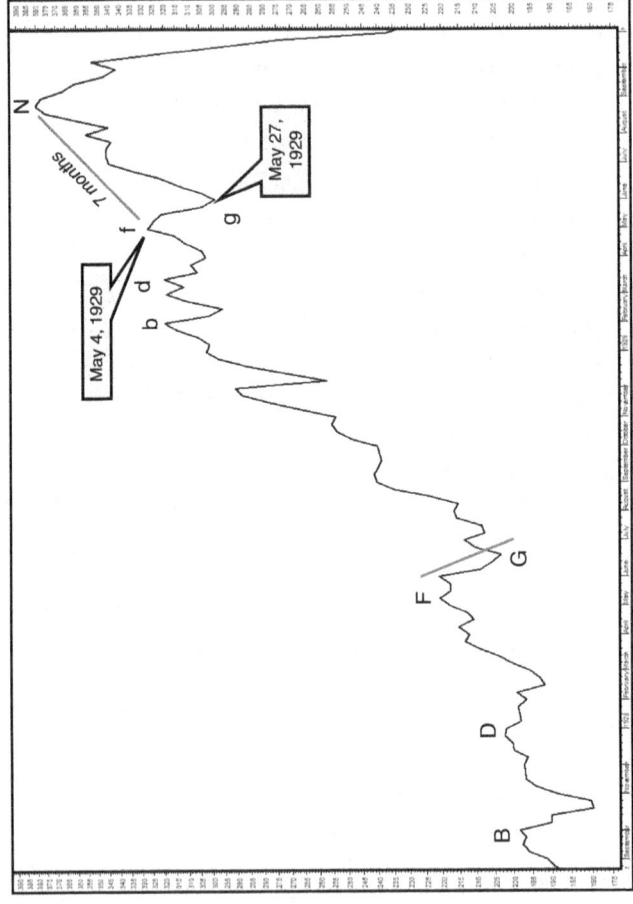

FIGURE 6.4 Tri-Day Method, Complex Arrangement. Chart created by MetaStock®.

From 358.42 subtract 19 (the loss in the Separating Decline), and the remainder is 339.42. This is the number of points that the Dow is expected to lose between points N and S.

Deduct 339.42 from 381.17 and the remainder is 41.75. That is the projected Tri-Day price at point S. The actual bear market low on July 8, 1932, was 41.22.

Conclusion

"In any given instance, the Tri-Day Method may prove more accurate with one average than with another. It is advisable to make each calculation in two or more averages."

Not all Three Peak patterns can be used to calculate a low. Some of them must simply be forgotten in the light of later fluctuations. *"Market history shows that a formation can be discarded (1) when it is supplanted by another pattern which precedes or follows it, (2) when it is short or imperfectly formed, or (3) when it occurs at a very low level, historically, in the average."* The more flaws there are in the shape and character of the pattern, the less confidence that can be had in the forecast.

The points F, G, K, L, M, N, and so on are to be applied to actual market fluctuations only in retrospect. If someone tries to locate them at the time they occur, he will almost surely be mistaken. It must be emphasized: Projections of point S can be made only after the entire formation is complete.

As soon as it is decided that the formation is a Domed House, it is known that the price average must return to the bottom of the Three Peaks, regardless of what the calculated price is.

Endnote

1. Unless otherwise indicated, all quotes in this chapter are taken from George Lindsay's self-published newsletter, *George Lindsay's Opinion,* May–September 1959.

Part III

The Lindsay Timing Model

Chapter 7: Overview of the Lindsay Timing Model 93

Chapter 8: Key Dates 103

Chapter 9: The Low-Low-High Count 119

Chapter 10: Combining the Counts 129

Chapter 7

Overview of the Lindsay Timing Model

"Most timing studies arrive at a decision to buy or sell through methods which have nothing directly to do with time itself. The procedure described below is timing in the literal sense of the word—merely counting the number of days....On its face, it is for short-term traders. But it can also benefit investors: they will simply use it less frequently."[1] –George Lindsay

In 1965, George Lindsay published a newsletter titled *A Timing Method for Traders*. The goal of this method or model is to identify tradable tops in the markets. Part II of this book, "Three Peaks and a Domed House," mentions that the Timing Model is the "concluding technique" of the 3PDh model. It also says that the Timing Model is a free-standing technique all by itself and is not in need of any other indicators or models. The tops identified by this model are not only the secular or cyclical bull market tops identified by the 3PDh model. The tops anticipated by the Timing Model range from bull market tops to tops followed by corrections of only a few days. Chapter 9, "The Low-Low-High Count," explains how the relative duration and depth of the expected correction can be anticipated. In honor of Lindsay (and in an attempt to give his model a less awkward epithet), this book refers to this work as "The Lindsay Timing Model."

Similar to the Three Peaks and a Domed House model, the Lindsay Timing Model can be used by serious traders or passive investors. *"The most casual use of the principles can be of some benefit."* And like the 3PDh model, the Lindsay Timing Model will yield additional insight to the user as he or she invests more time into becoming familiar with it and understanding it.

Lindsay wrote that the model can be applied to individual stocks, stock market indexes, and commodity futures. He also wrote in a different newsletter that this model doesn't work very well in a bull market. Experience has shown that Lindsay's comment was more the result of modesty than of accuracy. The model can prove quite useful in a bull market, particularly when used to confirm bearish, short-to-intermediate-term signals from other indicators. All his examples focused on the Dow Jones Industrial index, but it has been confirmed that the model works on a wide variety of asset classes. Lindsay claimed to have tested his timing model back to 1861. In this case, he explained that he tested the model prior to the inception of the Dow Industrials by computing a daily average of "seven market leaders" from 1861 to 1885.

Introduction to the Lindsay Timing Model

"Virtually every bull market high on record came at the end of a Top-to-Top count; and the key date, from which the count began, was sharply delineated on the chart."

The model itself is composed of three basic concepts:

1. The 107-day Top-to-Top interval
2. The Low-to-Low-to-High interval
3. The convergence of these two intervals, which gives us our targeted top or high

The Lindsay Timing Model is unusual in that while the cycle archetype attempts to identify time intervals between lows in price (that is, a 21-day cycle counts 21 days between successive price lows), Lindsay's approach to this particular interval uses price **highs.** A count of 107 calendar days from a correctly determined origin should be expected to identify a top in price (see Figure 7.1). The model allows for a ±5-day window on either side of the targeted date. In other words, the 107-day interval may be only a 102-day interval or it may extend to 112 days. Another difference between the 107-day interval and the archetype cycle that most readers will be inclined to think of is that the 107-day interval is not a cycle at all. It is really an interval of time. One should not expect a regularly recurring cycle of 107 days from this model. These "cycles" are more appropriately referred to as "intervals."

The Top-to-Top count is not from one high to another but from a **low** within a top (Range Top) to a top (the intraday high of an advance). The problem of semantics becomes increasingly clear.

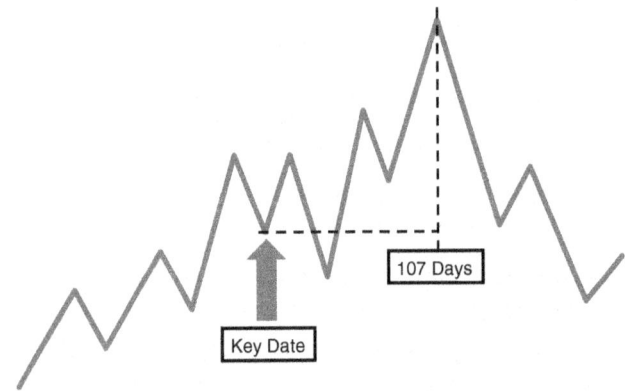

FIGURE 7.1   *The 107-Day Top-to-Top count.*

Once the key date is identified, it is an easy task to count forward 107 days to find the targeted date for the high of the advance. Counting is done with calendar days, not trading days. This becomes an easy task with the plethora of online calendars and date counters available free of charge on the Internet. The **targeted** date for the high often falls on the same date as the **true** high of an advance. Lindsay identified the high of an advance using intraday highs and not closing highs. He even went so far as to write, *"The high day at the end of the count is determined according to the intraday or hourly prices."* It certainly isn't necessary to use intraday or hourly prices to implement the Lindsay Trading Model. All examples Lindsay shared in his writing used daily charts.

The true high of the advance is expected to be contained within a 5-day window on either side of the targeted date. Therefore, we should expect to find the true, or intraday, high anywhere from 102 days to 112 days after the key date. Lindsay took the time to write, *"It is comparatively infrequent for a Top-to-Top count to last as long as 111 or 112 days."* He also explained that one exception to the preceding should be noted: A 107-day count can also expire at the end of a trading range or congestion on the chart. It need not be within the 5-day window if price has been contained within a trading range since the targeted high.

Once the target date of the 107-day interval is determined, the analyst will then attempt to find Low-to-Low-to-High (LLH) intervals that converge with it. The identification and creation of the LLH interval are explained in Chapter 9. For now, one need only understand that an LLH interval is composed of two equal time intervals, the first of which is between two price lows. The second interval is between that second low and a possible price high. A simple example of the LLH interval could be a low pinpointed on the first day of the month and another low found on the fifth day of the month. The time period between these two lows is counted as four days. Four days would then be added to the second low to identify a potential high on the ninth day of the month. Clearly, counting forward a number of days found between two lows doesn't always identify a high in price. What the model is trying to do, by combining the LLH interval approach with the 107-day Top-to-Top interval approach, is triangulate a short time interval in which a tradable top is expected to occur. One can think of the convergence of these intervals, during some window of time, as creating a mass that has its own gravity. The gravity draws the price upward until that point in time has passed. Once that point in time has passed, the convergence loses its gravity and the price begins to drop.

Most market timing models involve focusing on current market action. This common aspect of most indicators can cause the analyst or trader to feel pressured and to subsequently make a decision under duress. One of the many attractions of the Lindsay Timing Model is that the focus of the analyst is directed to past market fluctuations. This tends to relieve some of the pressure of being forced to make a decision today based on today's, or very recent, market action. For example, in the case of the 107-day count, the analyst has 107 days in which to arrive at his estimate. This is a nice idiosyncrasy of the model.

Modern readers will appreciate the fact that the counting in Lindsay's timing model uses calendar days rather than trading days. This enables the practitioner to use any one of a number of online (Internet) date counters and calendars to quickly count the number of days *("...merely counting the number of days")* between price lows in the past and to find the dates of targeted highs in the future.

Terminology

Semantics quickly becomes an issue when one is reading Lindsay. Many of the ostensibly simple terms he used apply to more than just one concept and quickly become confusing. For example, when Lindsay refers to a "top," is he referring to the targeted, final top of the advance, or is he referring to the top from which we measure the origin point of the 107-day count? Is the final "top" he refers to an absolute high in price or is this top the time span of the ±5-day window that encompasses the intraday high? These are all concepts that are simple to understand but need to be differentiated and labeled in order to understand and apply the Lindsay Timing Model. This book attempts to differentiate these simple concepts by adding a few terms to the conventional "Lindsay vocabulary." Readers who are not familiar with Lindsay's work will never notice these additions. Those readers who are already acquainted with Lindsay's work will, hopefully, not be distracted by the new terminology. Indeed, it is hoped they will find the additional categorization and labeling of concepts helpful.

A Few Simple Reminders

Everyone sometimes loses track of the forest while concentrating on the trees. When beginning one's study of the Lindsay Timing Model, a student would do well to remember this one simple dollop of common sense: In order for the model to call a "top," the market must be advancing. If the market had been advancing previously, a targeted date at the end of a trading range is acceptable, too. But sometimes the targeted date occurs during a market decline. Tops don't occur in falling markets! Don't expect the Timing Model to do the impossible. A falling market is an easy way to rule out the possibility of a top and thus is another tool to be used. That raises a question: How long must a market be advancing before a top can be called? The answer to that question has often been "less than a week."

It is suggested that one begin this process using a spreadsheet rather than marking up a price chart. While the result of marking 107-day intervals on a chart can be legible, the number of annotations required for the LLH model will make your price chart impossible to read. Even Lindsay didn't try to fit all the annotations required by the model onto just one chart. Rather, for his examples, he used two separate charts (one chart for the 107-day intervals and one for the LLH intervals). This approach still necessitated flipping back and forth between charts on different pages. Trying to match up dates on two separate price charts, while certainly not impossible, doesn't add anything to the learning experience other than a marginal level of frustration. Using a spreadsheet to list all the dates required of this approach is much cleaner and simpler.

Finally, if the analyst keeps his eyes peeled, he will notice that inflection points in the market can often be identified by the 107-day interval measured not just from tops but from bottoms as well. Also, LLH counts that fail to identify a price high may well have pinpointed a price low. These realizations may not help with implementing the model but do help to further the theory, and our understanding, of intervals **and** cycles.

Endnote

1. Unless otherwise indicated, all quotes in this chapter are taken from George Lindsay's self-published newsletter, *George Lindsay's Opinion,* during the years 1959–72.

Chapter 8

Key Dates

"This whole timing method depends on locating the key date correctly on the chart."[1] –George Lindsay

This chapter examines Lindsay's approach to locating the origin of the 107-day interval, the date from which we count forward 107 days. Lindsay referred to the origin as the key date. The targeted date for the high of the advance is 107 days after the key date. The true date containing the ultimate, intraday high of the advance is assumed to lie within a time window that extends 5 days on either side of the target date. Thus, the true date may lie anywhere from 102 days to 112 days from the key date. Somewhere in this 5-day window is the top of the recent advance. If this target date is not confirmed by Low-to-Low-to-High intervals, we shouldn't expect too much of a decline. Yet some sort of decline is often witnessed. The problem with putting too much emphasis on the time window without confirmation by LLH intervals is that we don't have a feel for where in the time window it is best to go to cash or to short the market. Without more assurance of a tradable decline emerging from a narrower time frame from which to time our trade, trading with nothing more than a 107-day interval can often be "less than profitable." A trader should not exclude other technical signals as confirming indicators, but that is beyond the scope of this book.

Key Range

"Most top formations are easy to recognize on a chart after they have been completed which is when we use them."

The key date (origin) is contained within a Topping Range, which we shall refer to as the Key Range. Lindsay used closing prices to find key dates and intraday highs to classify market tops. Look for the lowest closing price (not the intraday low price) when selecting a key date. In the preceding quote, the "top formation" Lindsay was referring to was the Key Range and not the target range 107 days later. It is probably easier to recognize a top formation than to define it. The closest Lindsay came to defining a Key Range was as follows: *"Prices move back and forth over the same range. The fluctuations can assume any one of a number of patterns—it doesn't matter which. When the average drops under the low of the whole range, a top has been completed."* Lindsay also wrote in one example: *"The five market days from July 10 to 16…constitute a minor top formation, since prices broke sharply for two days afterward and violated the previous minor low point."* This book identifies a Key Range by finding a new high followed by a retracement to a low that is lower than the final correction preceding the identified top (see Figure 8.1).

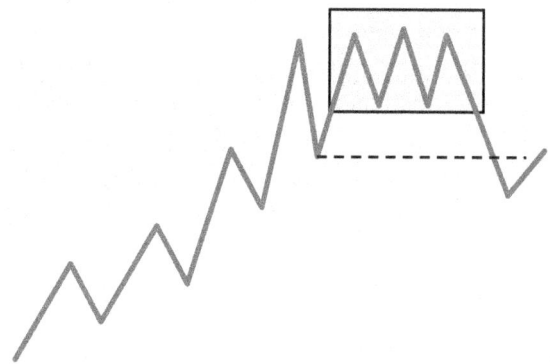

FIGURE 8.1 *Key Range.*

Broadly speaking, there are two types of Key Ranges:

- Compact Top formations
- Major Top formations

Compact Tops are the most common of the top formations. Major Top formations extend over a multi-month period and are likely to contain several Compact Top formations. Once Compact Tops are understood, Major Top formations are intuitively obvious—nothing more than a big Compact Top.

Compact Top Formations

"The low day of the most obvious dip in a top formation is the key point. This is where every Top-to-Top count begins."

There are nine variations of this common framework of the Key Range, as examined next. Once the particular variation is identified, finding the key date is straightforward and fairly simple, though it sometimes requires a bit of artistic license and flexibility on the part of the analyst. Lindsay's background as an artist is apparent because many of his methods require the analyst to interpret and get a "feel" for what the market is doing as opposed to insisting that the market fit into any preconceived formulas.

Double Top

The Double Top formation is the best formation to begin an examination of top variations because it is the simplest.

"Whenever there is a well-defined double top, or approximate double top, the low day of the dip between the two peaks is nearly always the correct key date." (See Figure 8.2.)

The low date in a top formation can be thought of as the "center of gravity" of the Topping Range. Thinking in these terms may help the student to get a feel for what Lindsay was attempting to do in identifying key dates. Examples of counts from Double Tops can be found in Table 8.1.

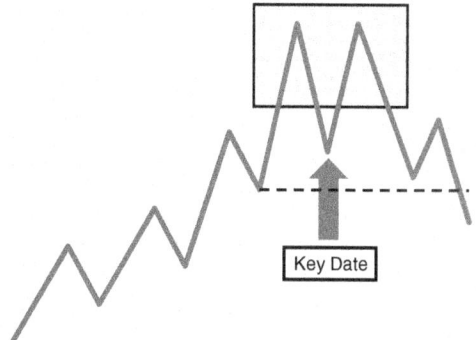

FIGURE 8.2 *Double Top.*

TABLE 8.1 *Top-to-Top Counts at Bull Market Highs: Double Top Formations*

Low	Days Elapsed	Market Top
6/14/1912	108	9/30/1912
7/27/1938	108	11/12/1938
2/27/1948	108	6/14/1948
12/15/1955	113	4/6/1956
4/23/1959	102	8/3/1959
9/24/1961	111	12/13/1961

Double Bottom Top

"When the dip ends at a double bottom...the first low is nearly always the correct one."

When there are two or more dips of approximately equal depth in a top formation, the key date (from which we count) is likely to be the first of them. It is also likely to be the dip that comes before the highest point of the whole top formation. These characteristics are generally, but not invariably, true (see Figure 8.3).

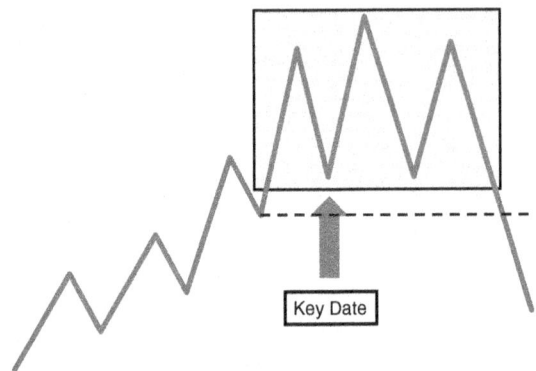

FIGURE 8.3   *Double Bottom.*

Head-and-Shoulders Top

Given Lindsay's comments on Double Bottoms (previously), one shouldn't be surprised by his approach to Head-and-Shoulders Tops: *"When there is a Head-and-Shoulders Top, the key date is the low of the decline that comes after the left shoulder and before the head."* (See Figure 8.3.)

Finding the key date in Double Bottoms and Head-and-Shoulders Tops is a good example of the need to get a feel for the market. Is the key date the first dip or the second dip? Luckily, a simple solution is to count from both dips. This simple solution is sharpened up using the examination of Low-Low-High intervals in Chapter 9, "The Low-Low-High Count."

Final Dip

A Final Dip is not a Key Range. The last dip before the end of an advance often functions as the key date when there is no Key Range to guide us. This is an extremely common situation (see Figure 8.4). *"When a top formation is neither a head-and-shoulders nor a double (or triple) top, prices usually remain close to the highest point only a very short time....In such cases, the key date is nearly always the last dip on the way up to the high. There was no dip worthy of the name in those five days. When this is true of any top pattern, we go back to the last minor dip on the way up to the high. The dip may last one day or several. The low day of that dip becomes the key date."*

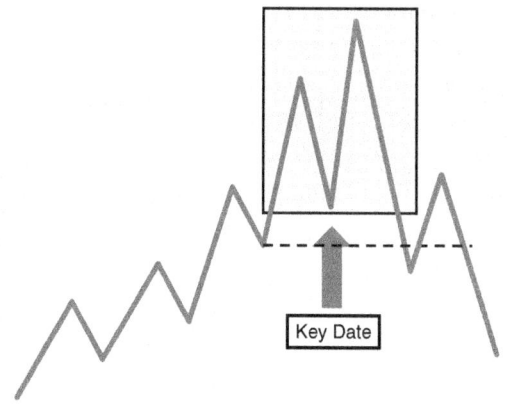

FIGURE 8.4 *Final Dip.*

In referring to key dates composed of Final Dips, Lindsay wrote: *"They were sell-offs lasting about one day which came only two or three days before the final high of the advance. Others—like those of December 1952 and May 1959—were declines lasting four or five days, which came from one to three weeks before the final high. Thus, a certain amount of discretion is involved in selecting the last dip on the way up to the high."*

Range Dip

One key date variation that Lindsay alluded to, almost in passing, but didn't attempt to categorize is similar to the Final Dip. It actually is a Final Dip if, rather than defining it as the *"last dip on the way up to the high"* trading day, one thinks of it as the last dip prior to the Key Range.

*"The five market days from July 10 to 16, shown at point 9, constitute a minor top formation, since prices broke sharply for two days afterward **and violated the previous minor low point.**"* The "previous low" Lindsay referred to ended up being a key date itself (see Figure 8.5).

Using a Range Dip in conjunction with a Final Dip can narrow the target range and provide a higher level of confidence in the target date. The final high of a move often falls between target dates measured from these two key dates. Care must still be taken to use LLH intervals, however. LLH intervals are explained in Chapter 9.

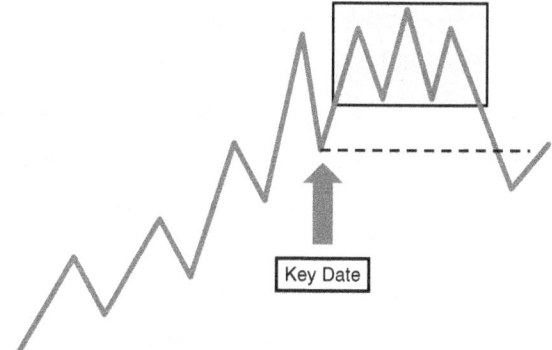

FIGURE 8.5 *Range Dip.*

Bottom to Top Counts (BTC)

"They are of the same duration as Top-to-Top Counts and are frequently found in long bull markets. But they begin at any sort of bottom, not just at the low point within a top formation. They are much less likely to result in a big decline than a true Top-to-Top Count."

Bottom to Top Counts, or BTC, occur fairly frequently. They are the simplest of all key dates to recognize because one need not bother identifying a Key Range. They are nothing more complicated than counting forward 107 days from a bottom to a possible top. Look for these counts when markets exhibit an extended rise. Or rather, start counting from recent bottoms **during** an extended rise. When an analyst starts asking himself, "Where **IS** the Key Range?" chances are the BTC is the appropriate count to be considering. When a key date does not fall within a Key Range, then the market decline following the 107-day count is unlikely to be anything greater than of intermediate scope (see Figure 8.6).

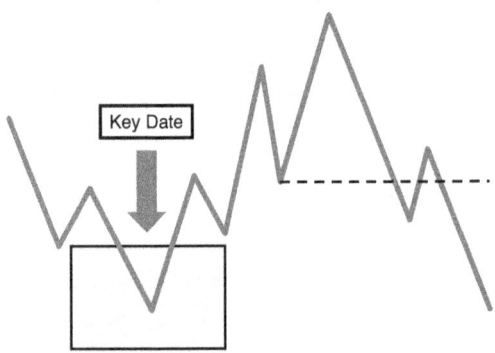

FIGURE 8.6   *Bottom to Top*

Special Class

"When a count can be taken from the primary low of a decline, the same type of count may also be taken from a secondary low which follows shortly afterward at a slightly higher level."

Closely related to the Bottom to Top Count is a category Lindsay referred to as a Special Class. Lindsay explained that 107-day counts could be taken from either of the dips after the key date in Figure 8.6. Counting forward 107 days from either of those subsequent dips takes one to a ±5-day window in which a bounce should be expected in the downtrend from the high counted from the primary low. This is similar to key dates in Major Tops (see Figure 8.9). A key date in a Major Top will time the start of a bigger decline that gets underway from a lower level. The count from the second key date in a Major Top is not used to identify a new high. This identified "high" should be expected to be a short-lived bounce and a point from which to expect a renewed decline.

Post Top Counts (PTC)

"There are, however, instances when the key date comes after the highest point, even though there was a possible key date prior to it."

The PTC is distinguished by the true key date appearing after the high of the Key Range (see Figure 8.7). A PTC is a less frequent phenomenon than the other variations examined previously. It should be thought of as an anomaly but not forgotten. The top in 1929 (September 3rd) was 113 days from the key date of May 13, 1929. The key date in May of 1929 occurred after the high of the Key Range. The 113 days is unusual in that it was outside of the 102-to-112-day target range, but the decline following the target date was unusual as well. Examples of Post Top Counts can be found in Table 8.2.

TABLE 8.2 *Post Top Counts at Bull Market Highs*

Low	Days Elapsed	Market Top
7/21/1919	105	11/3/1919
5/13/1929	113	9/3/1929
11/23/1936	107	3/10/1939
2/13/1946	105	5/29/1946
4/25/1956	106	8/9/1956

One would be wise to wonder how it can be known which dip in a Key Range is appropriate when this exception is always possible. The use of the Low-Low-High interval holds the answer to solving this riddle; it is explained in Chapter 9.

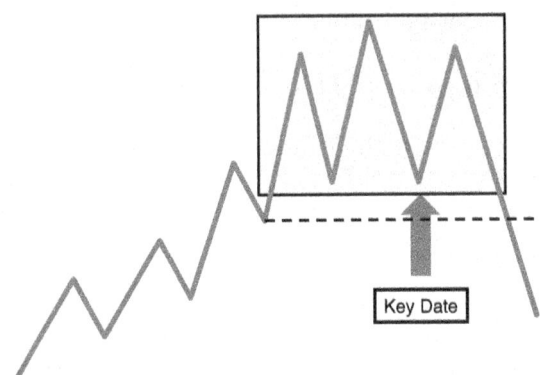

FIGURE 8.7   *Post Top Count.*

Sinking Key Range

The Sinking Key Range concept might seem confusing in a chapter concerning Top-to-Top counts, but it is not all that difficult. In an extended downtrend, a market is not going to develop a Key Range that fits the stereotype, but it normally will see periods of consolidation during the decline. It is during these consolidations we can look for key dates (see Figure 8.8). Often, the key date will take the form of a Post Top Count as the market will experience a substantial bounce after an extensive decline, pull back from the bounce printing the key date, and then bounce again but not as high as the original bounce. This consolidation is then followed by a renewed decline and prices dropping to new lows. This behavior would cause a key date to appear after the high of the consolidation, and the ensuing count is referred to as a Post Top Count. In this case, the PTC appears in a Sinking Key Range.

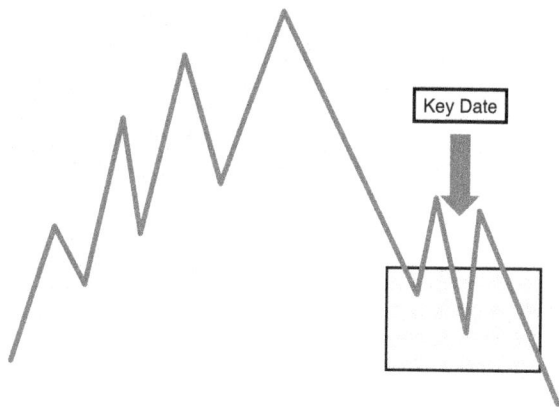

FIGURE 8.8 *Sinking Key Range.*

Major Top Formations

"The second kind of top formation is the long drawn out one....Each formation of this type usually has two key dates....Note that these key dates are found far below the highest level of the whole top pattern. A Top-to-Top count must be taken from both of the key dates in such a formation. The count from the first one is sometimes unimportant, or doesn't work at all....The count from the second date...is usually important and results in a deep decline."

Major Top formations tend to extend over a multi-month period and are likely to contain several Compact Top formations. A Major Top can be identified using the concept of the Range Dip (see Figure 8.9).

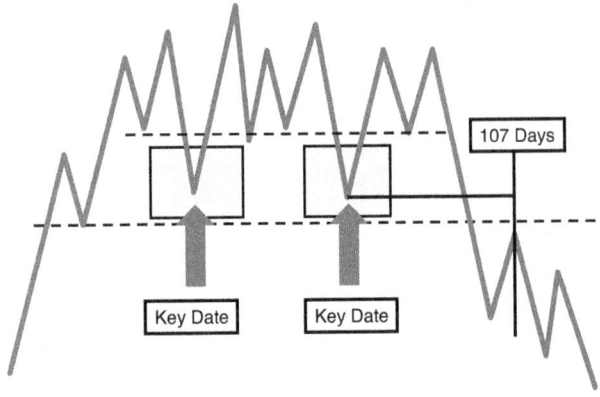

FIGURE 8.9   *Major Top.*

A key date in a Major Top formation will most likely need to be far under the highs of such a large Key Range. This is needed in order to identify the key date just as in a Compact Top. A key date in a Major Top will time the start of a bigger decline that gets underway from a lower level. It may be that the targeted top is the same, original bounce in the consolidation mentioned in the Sinking Key Range example previously. The count from the second key date in a Major Top is not used to identify a **new** high. This identified "high" should be expected to be a short-lived bounce and a point from which to expect a renewed decline.

Conclusion

Topping Ranges are composed of Compact Tops and Major Tops. The two types of tops are differentiated by the length of time involved in their construction and the fact that Major Tops usually contain several Compact Tops.

This chapter has identified and labeled the nine types of Compact Tops that Lindsay wrote of either explicitly or implicitly.

In contrast to Compact Tops, Major Tops extend over several weeks and can be easily missed if the analyst isn't looking for them. The primary use of Major Tops is to identify a point where an extended decline below the Major Top, or Topping Range, is to be renewed and can be expected to lead to an even larger decline than what has already been witnessed.

Endnote

1. Unless otherwise indicated, all quotes in this chapter are taken from George Lindsay's self-published newsletter, *George Lindsay's Opinion,* during the years 1959–72.

Chapter 9

The Low-Low-High Count

"Low-Low-High Counts are usually accurate within a margin of one or two days. This is their point of superiority. Many seem to work to the exact day, or even hour." –George Lindsay

In the Lindsay Timing Method, the Low-Low-High Count (referred to as LLH) is used to confirm the 107-day Top-to-Top count. Using the LLH interval count sharpens up the 107-day count considerably by eliminating less-than-ideal 107-day counts. The concept is quite simple. One begins by first determining the number of days between any two "lows," then counting forward the same number of days to arrive at a high (see Figure 9.1). *"The indicated high may be either the last day up or the first day down."*[1] The operative word in Lindsay's quote is "indicated." A high is not always the result of using this procedure in isolation, but even when no high is produced the method is still useful. By combining the LLH count with the 107-day count,

Lindsay developed a system that does a remarkable job of predicting highs in price. Sometimes the changes in trend predicted by the model are more severe than at other times. Lindsay gave suggestions to help determine the relative degree of a sell-off an analyst should expect, and they are included at the end of this chapter.

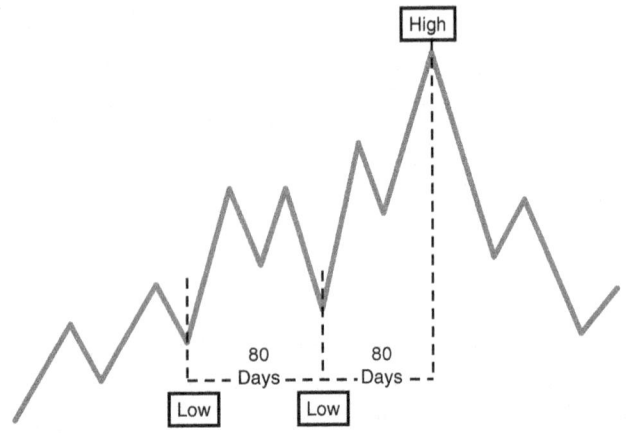

FIGURE 9.1   *Low-Low-High Count.*

Like 107-day counts, LLH counts are made using calendar days, not trading days. When one is using calendar days, the indicated date of a high sometimes falls on a Saturday, Sunday, or holiday. To determine whether the targeted high should be expected to fall on either the day before or the day after a closed day in the market, Lindsay suggested checking by counting market days. Fortunately, it has been found that the simpler process of assuming a Friday target date for counts ending on a Saturday and a Monday target date for counts ending on a Sunday works quite well.

Determining Lows

Before the analyst can begin counting, he or she must determine from which lows the counts will be made. Like key dates in the 107-day Top-to-Top count, lows are determined by closing prices. *"In deciding which day is the low, we go by closing prices with very few exceptions."* One exception Lindsay noted was for what he described as "extreme" intraday lows. Here again, he failed to define exactly what should be considered an "extreme" intraday low and depended on the reader's judgment. At one point, he wrote that that it would *"violate common sense"* to call one particular day the low just because it was the closing low when an adjacent day contained an extreme intraday low.

"A count can be taken between any two lows, no matter how far apart they are, or what fluctuations take place between them. Thus, there are an enormous number of Low-Low-High counts. Since we are interested only in worthwhile downtrends, we use a small number of the total counts. They must therefore be sorted out systematically to avoid confusion." The "system" Lindsay used to sort the lows was to differentiate between what he categorized as important lows and minor lows.

"First minor lows must be differentiated from important lows." Minor lows are easy to identify as they are any low other than an important low. Unfortunately, Lindsay doesn't define important lows. The closest he came to defining important lows and minor lows is when he wrote, *"The distinction should be clear from glancing at the chart."* For the purposes of this book, we shall define an important low in an

uptrend as a retracement that drops lower than a previous low in the uptrend prior to the most recent high (similar to finding a Key Range). An important low can also be thought of as a change in trend from down to up. As for downtrends, all the examples of important lows presented by Lindsay in downtrends appear to be forms of the "extreme" intraday lows discussed previously. He also wrote that a *"violence of fluctuations"* can cause an important low. A violent fluctuation would be expected to print an extreme (intraday) low. In this book, a major low in a downtrend is a low that precedes an upward retracement that climbs higher than a previous upward retracement found in the same downtrend.

Counts

Once the important lows and minor lows have been identified on a price chart, counting the intervals between lows can begin and the resulting counts and dates recorded in a log. Here, Lindsay distinguished between important counts and minor counts. He also took care to explain how long each type of count should be expected to have an effect on the market—that is, the longest interval the analyst needs to track for each type of count. There are four separate counts to be aware of: two important counts and two minor counts.

Important Counts

A count from one important low through another important low is rated as an important count. An important low has a maximum life of two years. *"For that long after it is established, take counts between it and every other important low."* This means that an important low can be expected to have an effect on the market for the next four years because counting forward two years from a second important low (identified two years after the first important low) would cover a total of four years. Of course, it is only those dates that are pinpointed by the counting, and not the time between the dates, that are important to bear in mind.

A count from an important low through a minor low also rates as an important count provided that the minor low is **not more than three months later.** This three-month rule eliminates what could have become an overwhelming number of important to minor counts during the preceding two years.

Minor Counts

A count from one minor low through any other minor low is rated as a minor count.

A count from a minor low to an important low is also a minor count.

The number of minor counts is kept manageable by the fact that a minor low is valid for **no more than four months.** *"During that period, take counts between it and every other low, whether important or minor."*

"Several counts are often made through the same low." A count can be taken between any two lows no matter how far apart they are. The reader can easily imagine how this could become a terrible mess and that

a spreadsheet is a necessary tool—even more so once the 107-day counts are included. One's sanity is saved, however, by the time limits Lindsay placed on the counts.

Combining LLH Counts with 107-Day Counts

At this point, the 107-day counts have been determined, important lows and minor lows identified, and the different counts all taken and listed in a spreadsheet. Now the recorded data is examined to detect converging dates and dates within the same cluster. *"At frequent intervals, compare the list with the expiration of any future Top-to-Top counts which are apparent. Retain all minor counts which expire within about a week on either side of a Top-to-Top count. Keep all important counts which expire within five or six weeks of a Top-to-Top count."* That last statement should cause the reader to pause. It would seem to invalidate the ±5-day window of the 107-day count if dates as far as five to six weeks away are to be "dates of interest." Lindsay appeared to contradict this instruction himself when he wrote, *"Low-Low-High counts are usually accurate within a margin of one or two days—unlike 107-day cycles with their 5-day window. This is their point of superiority. In all other respects, Low-Low-High counts are less important than Top-to-Top counts."* If the LLH counts are to narrow our target range from a 5-day window to a 2-day window (on either side of the target date), then it is confusing how an important count five or six weeks away should be of concern. The chief function of an LLH count tells us whether the Top-to-Top count will last 103, 107, or 111 days. This confusion is cleared up in Chapter 10, "Combining the Counts," in a discussion of trading ranges. For now, it is important to be clear on Lindsay's basic guidelines.

Expected Size of the Decline

"A Top-to-Top count can be used alone. A Low-Low-High count cannot. Its only value lies in the way it combines with some other count. An important Low-Low-High count should theoretically result in a bigger decline than a minor one. But the extent of the decline depends on how closely the Low-Low-High count agrees with some other count."

To get a big decline in the market, the first requirement is that there must be a Top-to-Top count. The second requirement is that the 107-day Top-to-Top count either must approximately coincide with an important Low-Low-High Count, or, as an alternative, must expire while the average is in the same trading range. Lindsay calls this trading range a "cluster." The third requirement to expect a big decline is that a minor count must coincide with both the major count and the 107-day count. Lindsay never explained what a "big" decline meant to him. From his writing, one can assume that he meant a decline through which an investor would prefer not to stay invested.

A mild decline can be expected with a mix of a minor count and a 107-day count. This matchup is not expected to produce a decline of interest to anyone other than the most nimble of traders.

Lindsay did suggest an exception to his rule requiring a Top-to-Top count. He wrote, *"There are cases, however, when several Low-Low-High counts coincide. They may then be used without confirmation by any other kind of count."* That statement is explored more fully in Chapter 10.

Conclusion

The following is a quick summary of this chapter and can serve as a quick reference guide in the future for the reader:

The Low-Low-High Count is used to confirm the 107-day Top-to-Top count.

Important lows and minor lows must be identified and logged.

Counts must be taken between all important lows within two years of one another.

Counts are taken from all important lows to all minor lows not more than three months later.

Counts are taken between all minor lows within four months of one another.

Counts are taken from a minor low to any important lows not more than four months later.

A big decline can be expected only if a Top-to-Top count is present.

Endnote

1. Unless otherwise indicated, all quotes in this chapter are taken from George Lindsay's self-published newsletter, *George Lindsay's Opinion,* during the years 1959–72.

Chapter 10

Combining the Counts

"To get a big decline in the market, there must first of all be a Top-to-Top count. Second, the Top-to-Top count must either approximately coincide with an important Low-Low-High count; or, as an alternative, it must expire while the average is in the same trading range."[1] –George Lindsay

Lindsay created four[2] categories of how Top-to-Top counts might coincide with LLH counts, and they are presented in this chapter with examples. Not all categories should be expected to produce greater than marginal results. Some combinations are more effective than others. Recognizing the different categories in real time will aid in estimating the depth of an expected market decline. In his original newsletter, Lindsay used examples from 1961 and 1962. This book draws from his original examples. A list of all the Top-to-Top counts in this period can be found in Table 10.1.

TABLE 10.1 Principal Top-to-Top Counts Between August 1961 and March 1965

Key Date	Days Elapsed	Market Top
8/24/1961	111	12/13/1961
9/25/1961	109	1/12/1962
11/30/1961	106	3/16/1962
1/29/1962	106	5/15/1962
2/26/1962	105	6/11/1962
6/4/1962	106	9/18/1962
7/6/1962	102	10/16/1962
8/21/1962	106	12/5/1962
10/1/1962	106	1/15/1963
10/12/1962	108	1/28/1963
3/31/1964	108	7/17/1964
10/15/1964	112	2/4/1964
12/1/1964	104	3/15/1965

Coincident Counts

"When several counts jibe so perfectly we have the ideal setup for a sharp decline immediately." In this case, Lindsay was referring to counts expiring within 24 hours of each other.

The first task is to locate a Key Range (there are several Key Ranges in the time frame shown in Figure 10.1). The Key Range between May 31, 1962, and June 6th is an example of a Sinking Key Range (a consolidation in a declining market). This key date is an example of a Post Top Count (PTC) because we have identified June 5th as the key date but the high of the Key Range fell beforehand on May 31st. Counting forward 107 days from the key date targets September 20th. This targeted date is two days after the intraday or True High on September 18th, which is well within the count's five-day window. (As for the high of August 23rd, workable counts have been found for this high, but they don't coincide within 24 hours; hence, they are not "Coincident Counts.")

The next task in our example is to identify important and minor lows. The extreme intraday low on May 29, 1962, qualifies as an important low. There exist several important and minor lows between May 29th and the targeted date of September 20th. The analyst would be expected to take counts between all of them. The double bottom in late July is a good reminder to not succumb to the temptation of excluding any lows because the second low on July 25th is the low that completes the puzzle. Counting from the day of the extreme intraday low (May 29th) to the minor low in late July (July 25th) yields a count of 57 days. Counting forward 57 days from that minor low in July produces the date September 20th—the exact date produced by the 107-day count and within 2 days of the intraday high of the advance. This count is an important count because it originates at an important low.

Another LLH cycle points to our targeted date. The overt important low on June 25, 1962, counts 43 days to the minor low of August 7th. Counting forward another 43 days from the second low of August 7th targets September 19th, only 1 day after the date of the True High of the advance and 1 day before the 107-day count target of September 20th. Observe that Lindsay used the **intraday** low on June 25th in this example, but he chose the **closing** low of August 7th. In July, he used the **intraday** low, again using his exception for

132 George Lindsay and the Art of Technical Analysis

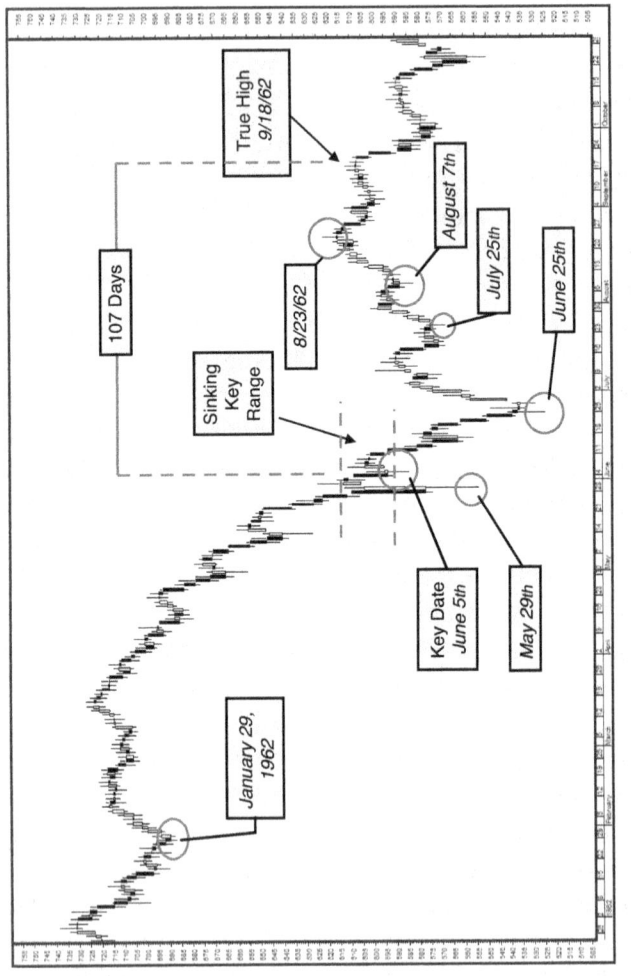

FIGURE 10.1 Coincident Counts. Chart created by MetaStock®.

"extreme" intraday lows. Comparing Lindsay's use of intraday lows versus closing lows begins to give the analyst a feel for what Lindsay considered "extreme" (since he provides no definition), but one should not fail to count through all lows.

Lindsay included a final example that does not belong in this category (Coincident Counts), but the reader would do well to examine it while focusing on this particular Top-to-Top count. This time he counts from the important low of January 29, 1962, and labels the closing low of May 28th (rather than the extreme intraday low a day later) as the second low—a count of 119 days. Counting forward another 119 days points to September 24th. This date is after the decline has started (hence, this LLH interval fails to target a "high") but is within the 5-day window of the True High. This is an example of how the second date in an LLH cycle may not necessarily be a "high" but can play a role in pinpointing a top.

Clusters

*"When the last count of a **cluster** expires, prices begin dropping at a faster pace—if an important decline is coming at all."*

For this category, Clusters, Lindsay used examples from the Major Top formation of 1961–62 (see Figure 10.2). Major Top formations tend to extend over a multimonth period and are likely to contain several

Compact Top formations as this one does. *"The second kind of top formation is the long drawn out one.... Each formation of this type usually has two key dates.... Note that these key dates are found far below the highest level of the whole top pattern.* Observe how far the key dates of September 25, 1961, and January 29, 1962, dip below the formation.

We begin by finding Key Ranges and the key dates within those Key Ranges. The most obvious key date of the Major Top formation lies in a Compact Formation/Double Top and falls on November 30, 1961. It counts 107 days to Monday, March 19, 1962. The True High was printed the previous trading day, Friday, March 16th. True Highs in a 107-day Top-to-Top count are determined by intraday highs.

After identifying key dates and target dates, important lows and minor lows are determined (using closing prices). The minor low of February 26, 1962, counts nine days to the minor low of March 7th. Counting another nine days forward targets the same date as the True High, March 16th. This is not an example of counts coinciding imperfectly because it is a perfect match with the True High and only a trading day away from the targeted date. A minor count, however, is not reliable without an important count to confirm it, and the following important count is an example of counts coinciding imperfectly.

Combining the Counts 135

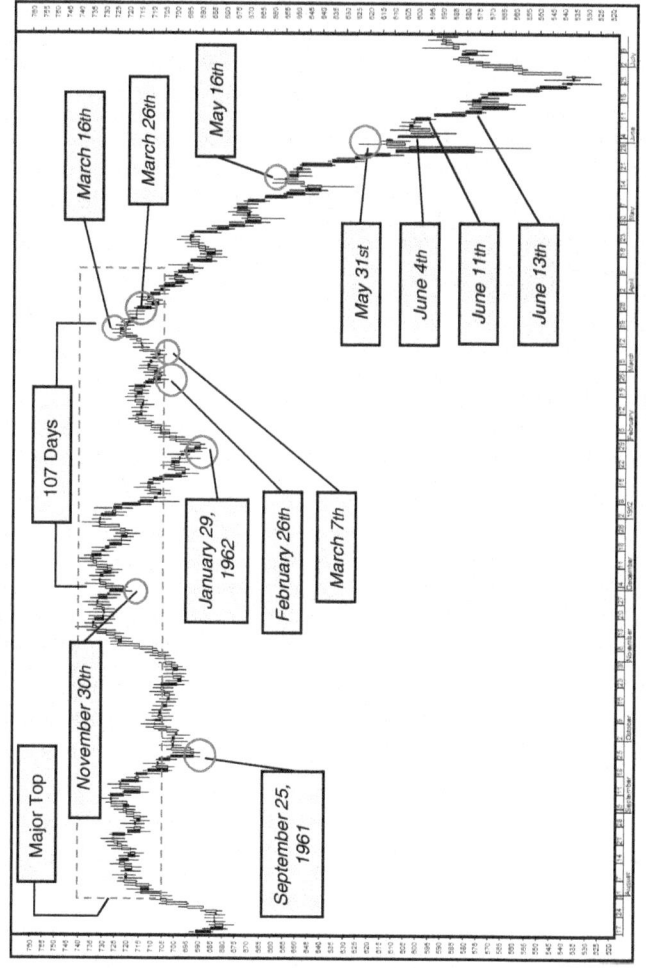

FIGURE 10.2 Clusters. Chart created by MetaStock®.

January 29, 1962, is an important low that counts 28 days to February 26th. Counting 28 days forward from February 26th targets March 26th. Lindsay called this imperfect convergence of a 107-day count, with minor and important lows, a cluster. *"But a Top-to-Top count must either coincide with some important Low-Low-High count, or else form a cluster with one."* In a cluster, the lows that have been identified need not fall in a symmetrical trading range but do need to remain in the same general area. A cluster seldom lasts longer than five or six weeks. A cluster requires an expiring important count, as do all successful target ranges. Lindsay described the price action of the Dow after the expiration of the Top-to-Top count as merely *"drifting off"* until March 26th, when the important count expired and the first significant decline occurred. *"When the last count of a cluster expires, prices begin dropping at a faster pace—if an important decline is coming at all."* Prices should drop in earnest once the final count in a cluster expires.

Additionally, in this Major Top, we see important lows on both September 25, 1961, and January 29, 1962. They should be expected to form an important count and are 126 days apart. Counting forward another 126 days arrives at June 4, 1962. This targeted date is within 2 trading days of the Sinking Key Range's intraday high on May 31st. June 4, 1962, saw a vicious break in price but no follow-through was seen until June 11th. Why was that? *"Prices never break shortly before a Top-to-Top count is due to expire."* Counting 107 days from the key date of February 26, 1962, pinpoints June 13th, putting June 11th within its ±5-day window. *"Prices always rise just before a Top-to-Top count ends."* When several counts combine, this characteristic could cause the range to become a nonsymmetrical cluster.

LLH Counts Only

"There are cases, however, when several Low-Low-High counts coincide. They may then be used without confirmation by any other kind of count.... A big decline within a short time normally occurs only after a Top-to-Top count expires."

Lindsay was quite definite about his rule that finding only one LLH count was worthless and that it must be combined with a Top-to-Top count. The chart Lindsay used is not included here as the concept is quite simple but bears repeating: *"A big decline within a short time normally occurs only after a Top-to-Top count expires."* His earlier statement asserts that a confluence of LLH counts without a Top-to-Top count may be used, but both his example and his statement make it clear that any expected decline will be abbreviated.

Trading Ranges

"When several important counts fail to coincide, but expire within a few weeks of one another, the result is usually a trading range. Whenever this is true, the presumption is that the average will fall under the lowest level of the trading range as soon as the last important bearish count expires—even though the exact day of the break may be determined by a minor count."

Lindsay made note of this idiosyncrasy at other times too—the tendency of price to hold up until the last minor count has expired. This characteristic applies to all categories.

Another universal characteristic that he felt was worthy of mention: *"When a key date occurs in a period of decisive price fluctuations [1/29/62], we can have more confidence that the resulting count will produce a deep decline."* A key date in a Major Top will time the start of a bigger decline that gets underway from a lower level. The count from the second key date in a Major Top is not used to identify a new high. This particular "high" should be expected to be a short-lived bounce and a point from which to expect a renewed decline. In Figure 10.2, counting 107 days forward from January 29, 1962 (the second key date in a Major Top), targets May 16th—1 day after the intraday high of the short consolidation found there. Lindsay also wrote that counts from the first key date in a Major Top are usually of no significance, but the count must be taken anyway because this is not always the case.

Conclusion

"Is it possible to determine in advance which one of the many Top-to-Top counts will result in a major bull market high? This problem has not yet been solved, but there are various ways of arriving at a partial solution, one of which will now be described."

Lindsay's "partial solution" was to explain the Cumulative Advance-Decline Line and then show examples of his Timing Model giving signals during divergences between the A-D Line and the Dow Jones Industrial index. *"According to our theory, the greatest probability of a major decline will come when there is a divergence between the Advance-Decline Line and the Dow Jones Industrials; and, at the same time, there is a clearcut, easily recognizable Top-to-Top Count."* Lindsay didn't mean to imply that this was the only method for determining a bull market top, just that it was a method, using a traditional technical indicator, that had worked well for him.

"Every technician dreams of one simple method which will always be an infallible key to the trend of the market. No single cure-all has yet been found. It is possible, however, to achieve a high degree of accuracy by combining several methods."

Endnotes

1. Unless otherwise indicated, all quotes in this chapter are taken from George Lindsay's self-published newsletter, *George Lindsay's Opinion*, during the years 1959–72.
2. Lindsay listed five categories, not four, but his fifth category, "The Top-to-Top Count in Bull Markets," was simply a review of what he had already written, with more examples.

Part IV

The Counts

Chapter 11: Long-Term Cycles and Intervals   143

Chapter 12: Basic Movements   161

Chapter 13: Counts from the Middle Section   189

Chapter 14: Case Study: The 1960s   203

Chapter 11

Long-Term Cycles and Intervals

"My version of cycles is different. I call them intervals. They are counted from a low to a high or from a high to a low. I project a movement to a point in the future which exists only in theory, the same as in cycles. But when I come to calculate the movement after that, I don't begin from the theoretical crest. I start counting from a high which the market has actually made. That's the difference between cycles and intervals."[1] –George Lindsay

Lindsay's counting method can best be described as a funnel approach. His analysis starts with a long-term interval that provides a wide range of time as a target. He then narrowed down that target using other, shorter intervals that provided shorter target time ranges within the larger ranges. During an appearance on Louis Rukeyser's television program *Wall Street Week* on October 16, 1981, when Lindsay was asked, "When do we get out of this bear market and into that bull market?" he replied, *"The end of the bear market; the earliest I can count it is about August 26, 1982."* The intraday low of the bear market occurred on August 9, 1982. The methods in Part IV, "The Counts," are those methods he used to make that calculation.

Long-Term Cycles

Long-term cycles were Lindsay's attempt at classifying the market's major lows throughout history. Figure 11.1 is Lindsay's characterization of the recurring pattern of each of three long cycles he believed the market exhibited between 1798 and 1949. There have been variations from one cycle to another but they were minor. Lindsay held that the essential pattern was remarkably persistent for 150 years. The **shape** of the patterns may appear differently in a chart but the **timing** remains the same. It is only the **shape** of the chart patterns that looks different.

The period from A to E lasts roughly seven years. It is an entity in itself. It is the first section of what he called the long cycle. Note that the two advances from A to B and from C to D are separated by only a shallow decline. Next comes a big decline from D to E. The low at point E is a dividing line.

The second section of the long cycle runs from E to M. The duration of the second section is variable, but is much longer than the first. As a rule, the 3PDh formation has occurred at the end of each long cycle. It runs from K to M, which is always a low of the first importance. The low following a 3PDh pattern, point M, then becomes point A to begin the next cycle. **Lindsay allowed for multiple (two, and sometimes three) long cycles to run simultaneously.** At any point in time, the cycles would be at different points in their progression.

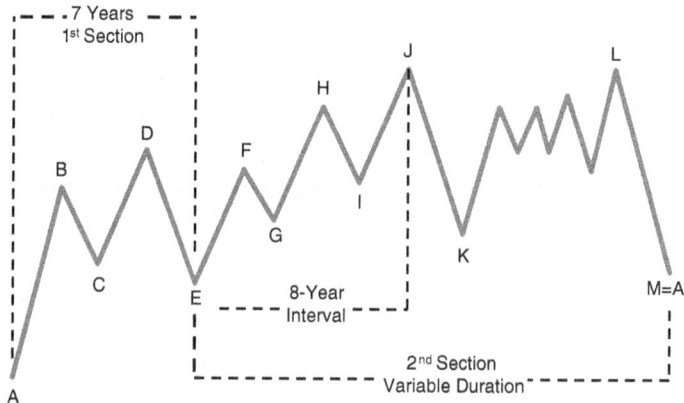

FIGURE 11.1 *Long cycle.*

The first two advances after point A are normally strong moves, and one of the two has invariably been extremely strong. Following point A in 1962, there were two very strong advances, the first ending in 1966 and the second in 1968. According to a different, simultaneous cycle, the 1962 low was point I. Advances following point I are only moderately strong. According to this strain, the next advance from 1966 to 1968 was to be the 3PDh formation.

Notice that the first (B–C), third (F–G), and fourth (H–I) declines are mild and the second (D–E), fifth (J–K), and sixth declines (L–M) are severe. All of the bear markets between 1949 and 1966 occurred when only one of two simultaneous cycles predicted a deep decline. This was true in 1957, 1960, 1962, and 1966. In each of these cases, one cycle indicated a severe decline, while the other showed a mild decline at the same time. Not until 1969 did both of the diagrams indicate a severe decline at the same time. That's why the 1969 bear market was the most severe since before WWII. Lindsay didn't expect another deep decline in the markets until 1977–78 (and again in 1980–81). It is not known how he responded to the decline of 1973–74.[2] Lindsay did correctly write, *"But a great change will come in 1975. From then until 1981, both lines will be relatively weak most of the time. There will never be any one year as bad as 1969 [obviously incorrect], but taking the five year period as a whole, the outlook is more bearish than anything the market has seen since the 1930's."*

Figure 11.2 labels two simultaneous cycles running from 1962 to 1982.

The long-term **cycle** pattern has one primary purpose: to recognize long-term **intervals.** There are three long-term intervals to keep track of. The first lasts 8 years, and it runs from a low to a high. The 8-year interval starts at point E and ends at point J. Remember that J may be lower than H. That makes no difference. An interval is not a trend. It need not end at the highest point of the whole sequence. The 8-year interval can start at any other points from A to M but occurs most frequently from E to J, C to H, and K to D. The latter two counts occur frequently but are not as reliable as from E to J.

Long-Term Cycles and Intervals 147

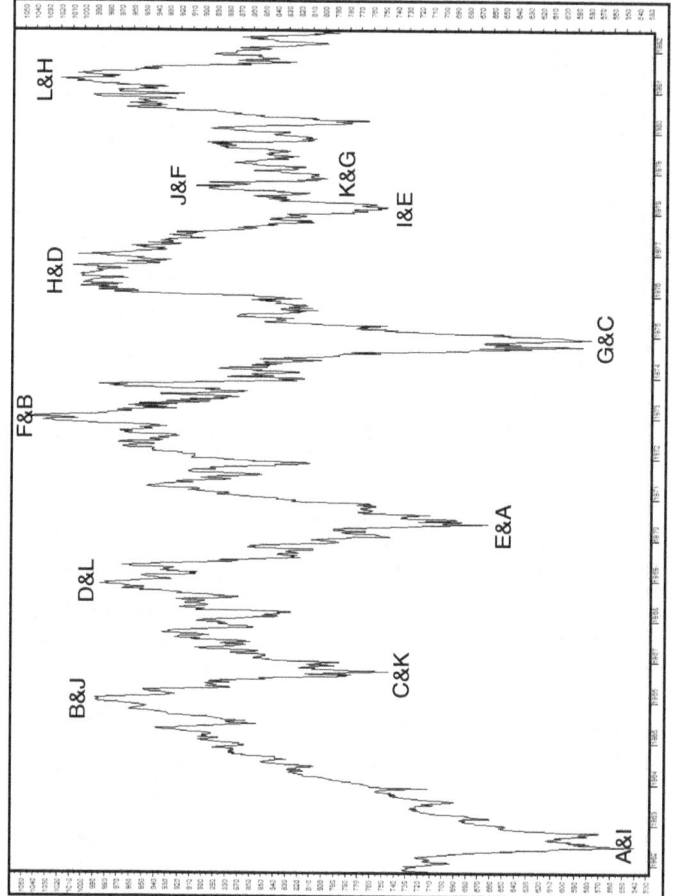

FIGURE 11.2 Long cycle. Chart created by MetaStock®.

The second long-term interval lasts 15 years and also runs from a low to a high. The elapsed time from A to J is normally 15 years. The span from point E to point D in the next cycle is also about 15 years, but in this position, the interval can stretch to 16 years. You can also count the 15-year interval from point K to point H in the next cycle.

The third long-term interval is the only interval of the three that runs from a high to a low. It varies between 12 years, 2 months and 12 years, 8 months. There are two high points from which it normally works quite well. That is, it is easy to recognize and ends at an important low. Count the 12-year interval from point D, and it usually ends at point M (see March 1937–June 1949). The 12-year interval also runs from point J to point E in the next cycle.

Long-Term Intervals

"But the intervals have been examined all the way back to the eighteenth century. The first one uncovered ran from 1798 to 1813."

An "interval" is simply the elapsed time from an important low to an important high or from a high to a low. It is called an interval because we ignore the fluctuations in between. It doesn't matter what its overall trend was while the interval was in progress, or **how many times it changed**, or **whether it ends higher or lower than the level at which it began**.

The two most important long-term intervals have always consisted of 15 years (from a bottom to a top) and 12 years (from a top to a bottom). The spans are not exact. The 12-year interval has **usually** varied between 12 years, 2 months and 12 years, 8 months. The latitude of the 15-year interval has been somewhat wider: anywhere from 15 years to 15 years, 11 months. All things being equal, 15 years, 2 months to 15 years, 4 months may be considered the norm. This does not mean that the **trend** of prices was up during a 15-year interval or down during a 12-year interval. An interval is considered down if it runs from a high to a low and vice versa. The relative level of prices at the turning points has no bearing on this matter. For example, a 12-year interval starts at a high and ends at a low, but the 12 years may have evolved over a long bull market and the ensuing low could be higher than the original high.

15-Year Interval

"The most important long-term interval lasts about 15 years, or somewhat longer. It is counted from every bear market low, and occasionally from an intermediate low which stands out on the chart of the average with more than the usual prominence. The 15-year interval always ends at a high of some sort."

We start counting 15-year time spans from any important low. There should be a high at the end of the count. The long-term intervals do not help much in fixing the exact time reversals. **Their value lies in estimating the importance of the next move.** An important high occurred on July 12, 1957. We know it was important because it appeared 15 years, 2½ months after the epochal low on April 28, 1942. These long intervals do not try to pick the exact "address" of a high or a low. Rather, they attempt to identify the correct "zip code." Sixteen years, 3 months was the longest 15-year interval on record, and 14 years, 9 months was the shortest.

"There is a latitude of 11 months or more between the shortest 15 year interval and the longest. One may ask "what good is a measurement so inexact that it may be off by as much as 11 months?" The answer is that the 15 year interval is used to gain perspective and not to determine exact timing. To narrow down the time span in which the high must fall, we compare the 15 year interval with the shorter-term counts."

As part of his Annual Forecast for 1972 (published in the *Stock Traders Almanac*), Lindsay wrote, *"One long-term measurement calls for a major top 15 years, or a little more, after the bear market low of October 22, 1957. It is a way of counting which has usually proved reliable, but it is not exact. Since this is being written in July 1971, sixteen months before Election Day, the more detailed timing methods are not yet available for use. But one of them can already be applied and it places an important high about November 10, 1972, thus coinciding with the 15-year interval and the election."* It is apparent, from Figure 11.3, that the high of the bull market came just shy of 15 years, 3 months after the 1957 low and only 2 months later than Lindsay's forecast based on a 15-year interval. Examples of the 15-year interval can be found in Table 11.1.

Long-Term Cycles and Intervals 151

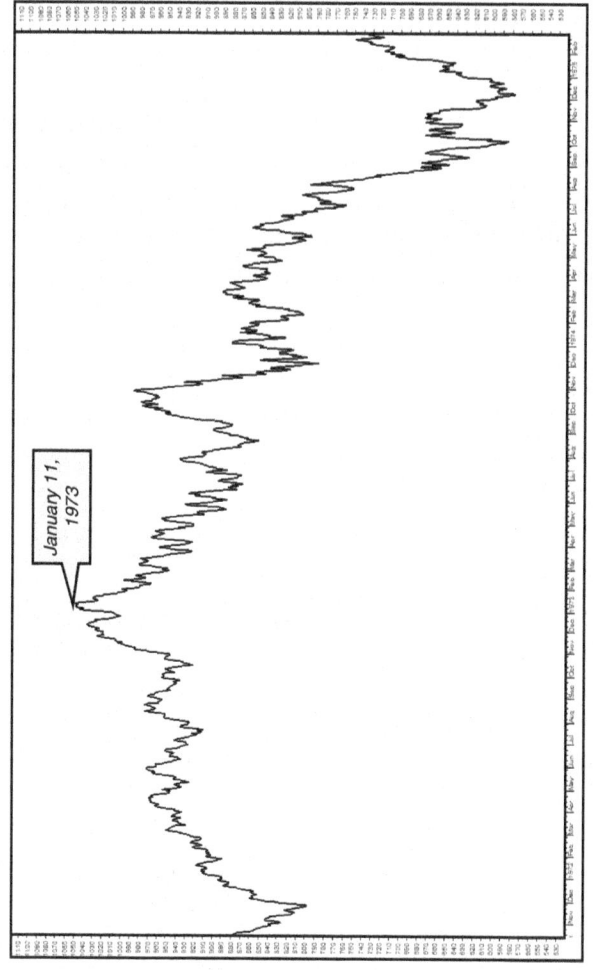

FIGURE 11.3 The 15-year interval. Chart created by MetaStock®.

12-Year Interval

The corresponding interval from an important high to a low is 12 years plus a few months. A low **usually** lies somewhere between 12 years, 2 months and 12 years, 8 months.

Examine the long-term interval from high to low that began on December 13, 1961. According to precedent, it should have ended not later than 12 years and 8 months afterward. That would place it in August 1974. There have been only two occasions in the past 100 years when it exceeded that duration materially. One was in 1970 and another in 1974. In both cases, the time elapsed was 12 years, 10 months. So, the low of 1974 came 2 months later than it should have. An overrun of 2 months is not excessive when we are referring to a span of 12 years or so.

Important: At a minimum, a 12-year interval is followed by a rally lasting seven months or a little more.

Figure 11.4 is a partial re-creation of a chart that Lindsay presented in one of his newsletters. It illustrates both the Principle of Continuity (when an upward interval of 15 years ends, a downward interval of 12 years must begin, and vice versa) and how multiple intervals are simultaneously functioning and overlapping.[3] See Table 11.1 for a sampling of 12-year intervals.

Table 11.1 is not meant to be a complete record of all long-term intervals during this period. This table is a collection of time spans found throughout Lindsay's writing. Some time spans appear to have been altered slightly by Lindsay as time passed.

Long-Term Cycles and Intervals   153

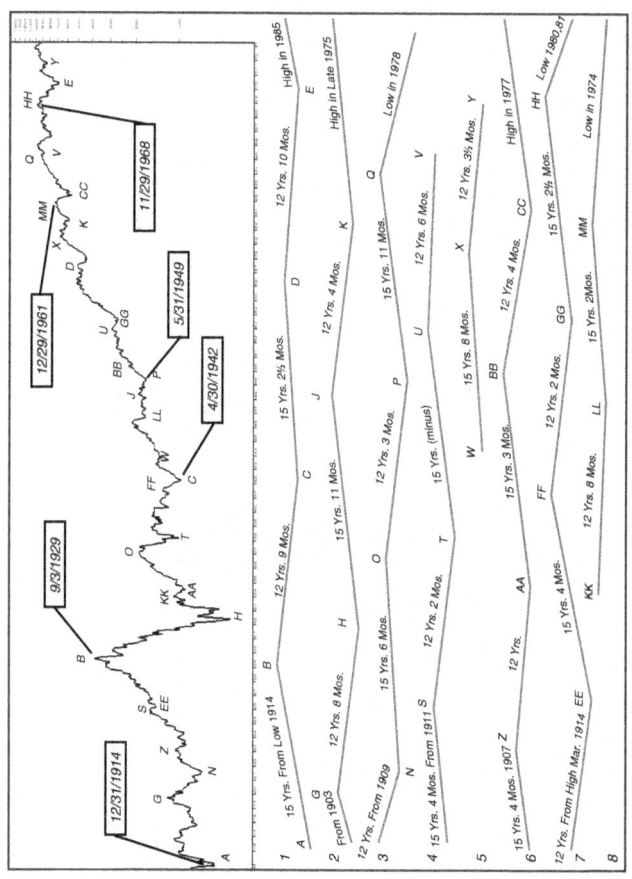

FIGURE 11.4 *Long-term intervals. Chart created by MetaStock®.*

TABLE 11.1 Long-Term Intervals

	Advances			Declines	
Low	Count	High	High	Time	Low
9/14/1914*	14yr, 11mo, 20d	9/3/1929	11/13/1919	12yr 8	7/8/1932
8/24/1921	15yr, 6mo, 14d	3/10/1937	3/20/1923	12yr	3/14/1935
8/27/1923	15yr, 16d	11/12/1938	2/11/1926	12yr, 1.5mo	3/31/1938
7/8/1932	15yr, 11mo, 7d	6/15/1948	9/3/1929	12yr, 8mo	4/28/1942
7/26/1934	15yr, 10mo, 17d	6/12/1950	2/5/1934	12yr, 8mo	10/9/1946
3/31/1938	14yr, 9mo, 5d	1/5/1953	3/10/1937	12yr, 3mo	6/13/1949
4/28/1942	15yr, 2mo, 14d	7/12/1957	5/29/1946	12yr, 2mo*	7/14/1958
11/30/1943	15yr, 8mo, 3d	8/3/1959	6/15/1948	12yr, 4mo	10/25/1960
10/8/1946	15yr, 2mo, 5d	12/13/1961	1/5/1953	12yr, 6mo	6/28/1965
6/13/1949	15yr, 11mo	5/14/1965	7/12/1957	12yr, 10.5mo	5/26/1970
7/13/1950	15yr, 6mo, 27d	2/9/1966	1/5/1960	12yr, 6.5mo	7/20/1972
9/14/1953	15yr, 2mo, 19d	12/3/1968	12/13/1961	12yr, 10m	10/4/1974
10/21/1957	15y, 3m	1/11/1973	2/9/1966	12yr, 1m	3/1/1978

* Curb prices: The New York Curb Market Association normally traded securities not listed on the NYSE outdoors on Broad Street, near the New York Stock Exchange. The association traded all classes of securities, however, during the suspension of NYSE trading in late 1914.

8-Year Interval

"If we count, not just from an ordinary bear market low, but from a really epochal bottom, there has always been a sharp break eight years later—a break so deep and rapid we can say that both an important high and an important low came within two or three months of each other. The crash of 1929 came eight years after the 1921 low. Eight years after the all-time low of 1932, the market really plummeted in May-June 1940, when Germany invaded France. The low of 1942 marked the end of a five year bear market, and stocks plunged in June-July 1950, when the Korean War broke out. The break of 1957 came eight years after the major low of 1949. When we count eight years from the low of 1962, we come to the spring of 1970, and again the market took a nose dive. The distinguishing feature of all these declines was not simply their depth, but the fact that an important high and important low appeared only two or three months apart."

The 8-year interval doesn't try to pinpoint bull market highs necessarily; rather, it attempts to find points at which a sizable drop should be expected. The targeted drop may be at the top of a bull market (1929) or it may be the last drop of a bear market (1970) or anywhere any in between (see Figure 11.5). There has always been a sharp break that lasts only 2 to 3 months, **and then a quick recovery that continued for some time, usually at least 5 months.** All of Lindsay's examples were contained within a period of 7 years, 9 months to 8 years, 2 months. A rule of thumb says to count 8 years to 8 years, 2 months. Although it is natural to use this particular long-term interval to help find market sell-offs, one should not overlook a point that Lindsay took care to emphasize: *"In every case, an important high and an important low appeared in the span of only two or three months."*

Some lows have the characteristics of both a point A and a point E in the long-term cycle. Eight years after one pair of these simultaneous lows, both a market top and bottom in rapid succession are found, and both of them are reversals of some importance. For example, 1929 came eight years after 1921, and the 1921 low had some of the characteristics of both a point E and a point A. There was a drastic break from September 3 to November 13, 1929. A strong advance began immediately and continued for five months. Thus, an important high (September) and an important low (November) both appeared just about eight years after the 1921 low. There are many examples of this. The spring of 1970 came eight years after the low of June 1962, which had some of the features of a point A and also a point I. Basically, any low in the long-term cycle, other than a low during a 3PDh formation, is usually followed by a high eight years later—provided that the low is decisively formed on a chart.

Long-Term Cycles and Intervals 157

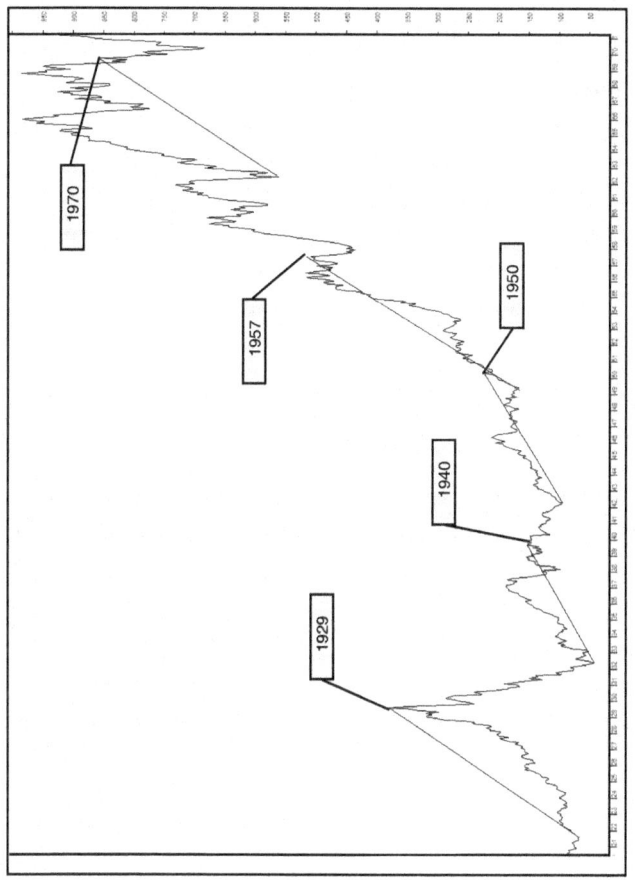

FIGURE 11.5 *The 8-year interval. Chart created by MetaStock®.*

The 12- and 15-year intervals are merely a way of roughly calculating the long-term probabilities of the market. They are not exact. There are two other ways of estimating future turning points on the basis of time alone. One is **Counts from the Middle Section,** which is covered in Chapter 13. The other is called the **Basic Movements** and is composed of the Standard Time Spans. They are called "standard" simply because approximately the same number of days has kept cropping up, time after time, throughout market history. The Standard Time Spans are not as accurate as the counts from the Middle Section (when they occur) but much more so than long-term intervals. The Basic Movements are covered next in Chapter 12.

Conclusion

The following is a quick summary of this chapter and can serve as a quick reference guide in the future for the reader.

Long-Term Intervals

It doesn't matter what the overall trend was while the interval was in progress, or how many times it changed, or whether it ends higher or lower than the level at which it began.

15-Year Interval

Runs from a low to a high.

The 15-year interval varies from 15 years to 15 years, 11 months.

12-Year Interval

Runs from high to low.

The 12-year interval has usually varied between 12 years, 2 months and 12 years, 8 months.

At a minimum, a 12-year interval is followed by a rally lasting seven months or a little more.

8-Year Interval

Runs from a low to a high and attempts to find points at which a sizable drop should be expected.

An important high and an important low appear in the span of only two or three months apart.

The 8-year interval has varied between 7 years, 9 months to 8 years, 2 months.

The sell-off is followed by a quick recovery that continues for some time, usually at least five months.

Endnotes

1. Unless otherwise indicated, all quotes in this chapter are taken from George Lindsay's self-published newsletter, *George Lindsay's Opinion,* during the years 1959–72.
2. Lindsay wrote the paper from which this information derives in 1970. He had expected points F&B to arrive in 1972, G&C in 1973, H&D in 1975, I&E in 1976, J&F in 1977, K&G in 1978, L&M in 1980, and M/A&I in 1981. The author has realigned the dates using Lindsay's Three Peaks and a Domed House method.

3. Lindsay mistakenly labeled point S, February 11, 1926, as 15 years, 4 months after the 1911 low when it was actually 14 years, 4 months. Unfortunately, we have no way of knowing whether recognizing this mistake might have affected his analysis. He also labeled point MM as 15 years, 2 months after the late 1946 low when it was only 15 years, and point CC as 12 years, 4 months after the 1950 high even though it was 12 years exactly.

Chapter 12

Basic Movements

"The underlying idea is that stock prices rise for approximately two years, decline for about a year, then rise for another two-year span and drop for a year. And so on indefinitely. The advances of two years, each one followed by a decline of one year, comprise what I call the medium-term counts."[1] –George Lindsay

A long-term interval provides a target range of dates but that range is very broad. *"But there must be at least one additional way of counting before any high or low can be established as of prime importance."* For more exact timing, we rely on the Basic Movements. Basic Movements (basic advances and basic declines) are composed of various medium-term counts, also referred to as the Standard Time Spans.

Medium-term counts (whose durations are given in days) and long-term intervals (of 8, 12, and 15 years) are two classes of intervals that must be combined in order to make a forecast. When two counts agree closely, it increases the probabilities of a severe decline.

When the end of a Basic Movement and the end of a long-term interval coincide in time, there is a decisive and often violent movement in the market.

The principal time spans are called "basic" and last anywhere from 10 months to three years. The reader has already been exposed to one particular basic advance in the 3PDh formation. Fortunately, the remaining basic advances and basic declines are much more straightforward and are characterized by the length of time (counted in days) for which the advance or decline persists. The duration of the Basic Movements varies but the variations have held within certain limits.

Lindsay's Rule of Continuity states that when a downtrend ends—either a basic decline or a long-term interval from a high to a low—an uptrend **of the same class** must begin immediately, and vice versa. We can always begin counting the standard basic durations from any basic high or low. We can also count Basic Movements from "important" highs and lows—the highs and lows that jump off the page at you.

Standard Time Spans

"People say, 'Times have changed,' or 'Conditions are different now.' Standard Time Spans have remained the same for 190 years. They have always been more nearly uniform than any possible arrangement of the price movement could be."

Standard Time Spans have been traced back to 1861 in detail and all the way back to 1798. They are called

Standard because the same durations have occurred over and over again. They are not identical, of course—they vary within certain limits because they are modified by short-term time spans (i.e., 107-day interval, 3PDh).

The counts that make up each category of time spans (long basic advance, short basic decline, etc.) are not identical, but they tend to cluster together. The numbers are not the same but vary only within certain limits. Throughout history, virtually the same numbers keep cropping up again and again. The Basic Movements method is based on this phenomenon of time spans.

Lindsay identified eight segments of time, which he termed Basic Movements:

Basic Advances	**Basic Declines**
Subnormal advance	Subnormal decline
Short advance	Short decline
Long advance	Long decline
Extended advance	
Sideways movement	

Basic Advances

An advance of about two years is followed by a decline of about one year or a sideways movement. A new advance immediately follows, and so on in unending succession. But the moves are not all equal in length or amplitude. Table 12.1 shows the variations in length. All 3PDh formations are "basic advances" but a basic advance need not take the particular shape of a 3PDh.

Note that a basic advance is often the same thing as a bull market, but it may also be only one section of an unusually long bull market.

There have been only three genuine advances that have been **subnormal:** those of 1932–34 (577 days), 1946–48 (615 days), and 1960–61 (414 days). (This observation of Lindsay's is very interesting because it tends to imply that other subnormal advances that he had listed in various appendixes were only temporary "working counts" used for educational purposes, as opposed to being his final count.)

A **short basic advance** is about two years or a little less and the average duration is 683 days. A short advance typically varies between 630 and 718 days. Most short advances continue for about 700 days.

The typical duration of **long basic advance** is roughly two years and two months or 775–805 days and has an average duration of 795 days. It varies between 742 and 830 days.

Extended basic advances are the longest continuous advances that are uninterrupted by a bear market. Extended advances range from 929 to 968 days and have an average duration of 953 days. No advance has ever exceeded the extreme of 968 days.

Prior to December 1972, there had been eight extended advances since 1877.

It should be noted that the maximum **sideways movement** is 348 days or 11 months. The highest point of a sideways movement can come at the start, in the middle, or at the end. The trend is suspended during a sideways movement. Examples of sideways movements can be found in Table 12.3.

Remember: When a basic advance ends, a new basic decline must begin on that same day.

TABLE 12.1 *Basic Advances*

Advances	Irregular	Short	Long	Extended
4/12/1877–11/12/1879				944
9/27/1880–9/15/1882		718		
*10/11/1880–9/15/1882		704		
1/17/1884–11/19/1885		672		
12/29/1884–12/3/1886		704		
4/2/1888–5/17/1890			775	
o-12/8/1890–1/21/1893			775	
7/26/1893–9/5/1895			771	
8/8/1896–4/3/1899				968
*6/23/1900–9/9/1902			808	
9/24/1900–9/9/1902		715		
6/23/1900–6/17/1901	357			
9/24/1900–6/17/1901	266			
10/15/1903–1/19/1906			827	
11/9/1903–1/19/1906			802	
11/15/1907–8/14/1909		638		
11/15/1907–10/2/1909		687		
7/26/1910–9/29/1912			796	
6/11/1913–12/27/1915				929
12/15/1913–12/27/1915			742	
12/19/1917–11/3/1919		684		
*12/21/1920–3/20/1923			819	
*5/20/1924–2/11/1926		632		
*1/25/1927–9/3/1929				952
*6/2/1931–7/17/1933			776	
7/8/1932–2/5/1934	577			
7/26/1934–3/10/1937				958
3/14/1935–3/10/1937		727		
3/31/1938–4/8/1940		739		
*5/1/1941–7/14/1943			804	
*4/24/1944–5/29/1946			765	

TABLE 12.1 Basic Advances (continued)

Advances	Irregular	Short	Long	Extended
9/6/1944–5/29/1946		630		
o-10/8/1946–6/14/1948		615		
6/13/1949–9/13/1951			822	
5/1/1952–1/5/1953	249			
9/14/1953–4/6/1956				935
10/22/1957–8/3/1959		650		
10/22/1957–1/5/1960			805	
10/25/1960–12/13/1961	414			
10/25/1960–11/15/1961	386			
*10/23/1962–5/14/1965				934
10/7/1966–12/3/1968			788	
1/30/1970–8/22/1972				935
5/26/1970–8/22/1972			819	
5/26/1970–1/11/1973				961
10/4/1974–9/21/1976		718		

o- Overlapping advances

* Secondary low

Table 12.1 is not meant to be a complete record of all Basic Movements during this time period. This table is a collection of time spans found throughout Lindsay's writing. Some time spans appear to have been altered slightly by Lindsay as time passed.

Prior to 1910, the rail average is quoted. After that date, the Dow Jones Industrials is used.

Prior to 1885, Lindsay used an index of seven market leaders that he computed from 1861 on, although there were gaps in it.

Basic Declines

The **subnormal** (or irregular) **basic decline** usually varies between 222 and 250 days and is always less than 300 days.

Short basic declines have varied between 317 and 364 days for an average duration of 345 days. The typical duration of a short basic decline is 340 to 355 days.

Long basic declines range from 376 to 446 calendar days. The typical duration of a long basic decline is 395 to 425 days or 13–14 months. The average duration is 408 days.

Lindsay made note of the tendency of basic declines to include two rallies in succession in roughly the same price range. Lindsay described the rallies during the basic decline from June 1931 to July 1932 this way: *"They were just the way the two rallies in the middle of a Basic Decline should look."* He also noted that the two rallies in the April 1930—June 1931 downturn did not occur in approximately the same price range as they theoretically should have. In the majority of cases, the two or three rallies make a series of descending tops.

The subnormal Basic Movement appears regularly in declines and only occasionally in advances. Most of the advances in market history have been of just about normal duration, while many declines have been irregular. While its count varies as much as the other Standard Time Spans, it is interesting how often the 221- to 224-day count appears. Readers will remember that this is the same count as is found in the 3PDh formation. *"The interval 221-224 runs all through history. It can extend from a high to a low, from a low to a high, from a high to another high, or from a low to a low."*

Remember: As soon as a basic low occurs, a new basic advance must commence immediately.

Whenever one Basic Movement is extra long or extra short, it is much more likely to be a decline than an advance. This is an important point to remember. There have been many subnormal declines. This is why so many of the basic declines have ended at secondary lows. There was a special reason for each one that could have been calculated ahead of time. Examples of basic declines can be found in Table 12.2.

In Tables 12.1 and 12.2, the figures represent the number of calendar days in the market's main movements since 1876. The time spans for both advances and declines are divided into four groups. The numbers in each column vary in length, but only within fairly narrow limits. All of the advances on record seem to have been cast from just a few molds.

TABLE 12.2 *Basic Declines*

Declines	Irregular	Short	Mean	Long
2/15/1876–4/12/1877				417
9/15/1882–1/17/1884				489
2/16/1884–12/29/1884		317		
12/3/1886–4/2/1888				486
5/17/1890–7/30/1891				439
o-3/4/1890–7/26/1891/3				509
4/18/1892–7/26/1893				464
9/5/1895–8/8/1896		338		
4/3/1899–6/23/1900				446
[1] 9/5/1899–9/24/1900				384
9/9/1902–10/15/1903				401
9/17/1906–11/15/1907				424
12/11/1906–11/21/1907		345		
[1] 10/9/1906–11/15/1907				402
12/11/1906–11/15/1907		339		
o-8/14/1909–7/26/1910		346		
11/19/1909–7/26/1910	249			
9/28/1912–12/15/1913				443
11/21/1916–12/19/1917			393	
[2] 11/3/1919–12/21/20				414
3/20/23–10/27/23	221			
3/20/1923–5/19/1924				426
2/11/1926–1/25/1927				
[1,2] 4/17/1930–6/2/1931				411
6/27/1931–7/8/1932				376

Declines	Irregular	Short	Mean	Long
7/18/1933–7/26/1934			374	
[2] 2/5/1934–3/14/1935				402
2/5/1934–9/17/1934	224			
3/10/1937–3/31/1938			386	
4/8/1940–5/1/1941			388	
7/14/1943–4/24/1944	285			
7/14/1943–9/14/1944				428
5/29/1946–5/19/1947		355		
6/14/1948–6/13/1949		364		
9/13/1951–5/1/1952	231			
1/5/1953–9/13/1953	251			
[1] 8/2/1956–10/22/1957				446
o-8/3/1959–10/25/1960				449
1/5/1960–10/25/1960	294			
11/15/1961–6/26/1962	222			
[2] 11/15/1961–10/23/1962		342		
12/13/1961–10/23/1962		325		
2/9/1966–10/7/1966	240			
12/3/1968–1/30/1970				423
[1] 5/14/1969–5/26/1970			377	
1/11/1973–8/22/1973	223			
[1] 10/26/1973–12/6/1974				406
[2] 10/26/1973–10/4/1974		343		
12/31/1976–2/28/1978				424
6/15/1981–8/12/1982				423

[1] *The basic decline starts, not at the high, but at the point where the average tries to regain its peak.*
[2] *The basic decline ended at a secondary low.*
o- *Overlapping declines*

Table 12.2 is not meant to be a complete record of all Basic Movements during this time period. This table is a collection of time spans found throughout Lindsay's writing. Some time spans appear to have been altered slightly by Lindsay as time passed. Prior to 1910, the rail average is quoted. After that date, the Dow Jones Industrials is used.

Prior to 1885, Lindsay used an index of seven market leaders that he computed from 1861 on, although there were gaps in it.

Soon after a basic high has been established and prices are on the way down, we watch for signs of a market low. As soon as a probable low becomes evident, note the length of time that stocks have been dropping since the last basic high. If the elapsed time agrees closely with one of the Standard Time Spans, it is accepted without question as a basic low. It doesn't matter whether that point is at the very lowest level of the whole decline or not. The practical rule to follow is this: When the market is falling from a high, watch it closely when the downtrend is between 340 and 355 days (the typical duration of a short basic decline) or 395 and 425 days (the typical duration of a long basic decline). If market action suggests that a bottom is being formed, accept that as prima facie evidence that a basic low is at hand. The same holds true for identifying market highs.

Once a Basic Movement (advance or decline) persists for longer than the extreme of that particular Standard Time Span, it should be assumed that it will continue until the next time span. For example, if what appeared to be a short decline has passed the 364-day mark, it should be assumed that it will continue until at least the shortest count of a long decline (376 days). Once a long advance continues longer than 830 days, it can be expected to become an extended advance that has a minimum length of 929 days.

The Principle of Alternation

The Principle of Alternation helps answer the question as to whether we should expect the next advance or decline to be long or short. Since 1798, when one decline was long, the next decline was short and the one after that was long, and so forth. There have been very few exceptions to this principle, and the same holds true of advances. (The 1973–74 bear market was an exception.)

Matching Basic Movements to Long-Term Intervals

By comparing the Basic Movements with the long-term intervals in the foreseeable future, it can be determined whether the current movement should be subnormal, short, long, or extended.

Matching Basic Movements to long-term intervals can also help us to determine the end of the current movement by deciding when the **next** movement should end. For example, if the current movement is a decline, then it must end in time for the next bull market high (15 years after a low) to arrive after a Standard Time Span. That is, the current decline must end soon enough for a basic advance (using the Standard Time Spans) to run its typical duration and be completed in the targeted time span of a 15-year interval.

Special Rule: Declines Following Extended Basic Advances

One normally starts counting a basic decline from the bull market top. In the case of a decline following an extended advance, however, a Special Rule applies, a rule that has worked consistently all through history: After an extended advance (lasting from 929 to 968 days), the basic decline does not begin immediately.

There is a preliminary sell-off, then an effort to regain the high. In Figure 12.1, the basic decline does not begin at the bull market high. Note how prices fell off from January to August in 1973, making several small recoveries on the way down. The average then made a concerted effort to regain its old high on the move from the August low to October 26th. The October high is commonly called the "Right Shoulder." As a rule, the Right Shoulder does not equal the bull market high, but there have been two cases when a Right Shoulder occurred at a level higher than the Head.

From Table 12.2, it is seen that short basic declines have varied between 317 and 364 days, for an average duration of 345 days. The low of October 4, 1974, was 343 days after the count from October 26, 1973—2 days prior to the average short decline and well within the typical range.

As an alternative, suppose we started counting a **long** basic decline from October 26, 1973. Long declines range from 376 to 446 calendar days. The average duration is 408 days. Counting forward 408 days from October 26, 1973, arrives at December 8, 1974. The Dow Industrials made their low just 2 days previously on December 6th.

How could we have known the peculiarities of the 1973–74 bear market ahead of time? The key to this enigma lay in the distance between the bull market high (the Head) and the Right Shoulder. If the distance between them is more than five months, the whole decline has often (but not always) been very long.

Basic Movements 173

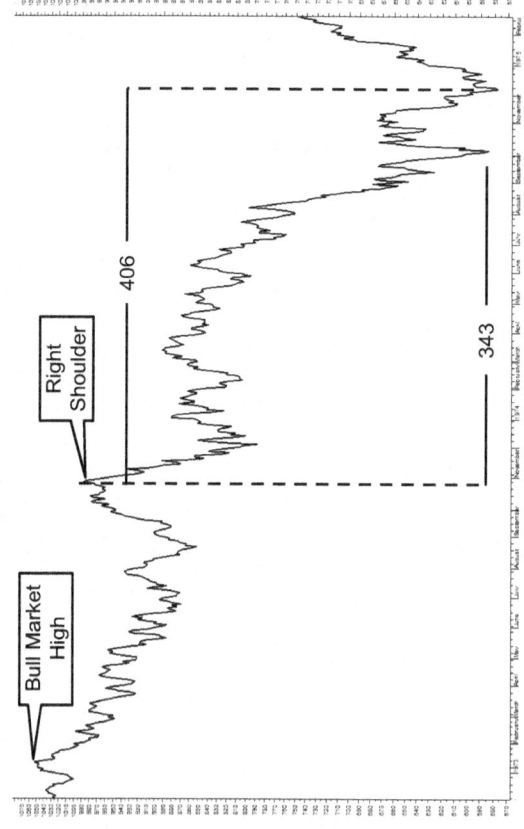

FIGURE 12.1 Special Rule. Chart created by MetaStock®.

See the following for examples of counts from a Right Shoulder:

Head	Right Shoulder	Months	Short Decline	Long Decline	Basic Low
1/19/1906	10/9/1906	9		402	11/15/1907
12/27/1915	11/21/1916	11		393	12/19/1917
9/3/1929	4/17/1930	7		411	6/2/1931
*3/10/1937	8/14/1937	5		386	3/31/1938
5/14/1965	2/9/1966	9	240		10/7/1966
12/3/1968	5/14/1969	6		377	5/26/1970
1/11/1973	10/26/1973	10	406		10/4/1974

* A bull market culminated after an extended basic advance on March 10, 1937, and it has a clearly defined Right Shoulder on August 14 of the same year. Yet in this case, the basic decline was counted from the Head and not the Right Shoulder. As a rule of thumb, the decline is counted from the Head when the elapsed time between the Head and the Right Shoulder is about *five months or less*. When the elapsed time from the Head to the Right Shoulder is more than five months, the probability is that we should count the next basic decline from the Right Shoulder.

Secondary Lows

"I am amazed because few technicians recognize that the length of time that market movements last has always been much more nearly uniform than the number of points which the averages gain or lose. Perhaps it is because, at least in my version of it, I sometimes start counting from secondary highs and lows. But such counts are made comparatively seldom."

The typical length of a major bear market has always been between 13 and 14 months. Some are shorter and sometimes it lasts longer, but the segment of the downtrend that comes after the 14-month limit has been brief. No matter how long it lasts, there is usually an obvious low between 13 and 14 months after the bull market high—*"not just any secondary top or bottom. But the secondary high or low, the one that fairly jumps out at you from a bar chart."* When this is the case, that low becomes the important one. This need not be the lowest point of the whole bear market. It must simply be an obvious low that stands out on a chart. We must start counting the next advance from the low that occurs around month 13 or 14.

When a **bear market lasts more than 14 months** (in response to a long-term interval that does not, and cannot, coincide with the basic low), we still count from the low that came 13 or 14 months after the previous high. The low at the 13th or 14th month is the key in establishing the continuity. Every time the 13/14-month low has occurred prior to the ultimate bottom, the length of the following long basic advance has varied between 775 and 805 days. In this case, the duration of any rally after month 13/14 is variable; it can continue as long as 5 months. The duration of the rally is a relatively minor matter. The important part is this: Once the period of rallies ends and the market again turns down, the active part of the remaining decline has always been brief—not more than about 3 months. The decline leading down to a secondary low has rarely lasted longer than 101 days.

Sometimes the bear market will last only 8 or 10 months and there is no well-defined low at the month 13/14 at all. In that case, we must use the low as it occurs and let it go at that. This was the case in 1966 when the bear market lasted only 8 months and there was never a clearly defined secondary bottom after that.

While basic declines have often ended at a secondary low, a basic advance nearly always ends at the extreme top. The need to use a secondary high as the top of a basic advance has occurred only once in the past 80 years.

Secondary Low Sequence

Focusing on the direction and time of the market, rather than the number of points gained or lost, the pattern following every one of the secondary lows has been very similar. Figure 12.2 is a composite of the formations that have been completed so far.

Point 1 represents the end of a standard basic decline, whether long or short. According to Lindsay's Rule of Continuity, it automatically becomes the low of a new basic advance. Point 2 is the top of the first rally after it. Point A represents the break to a new low. The move from point A to point 3 always took the average well above the level of point 2. After point 3, there has always been a rather deep decline (by intermediate trend standards) to point 4. From point 5 onward, there has always been an extended period of very narrow fluctuations. The period both just before point 5 and just after has always been marked by slow and halting movement. Point 5 goes only slightly above point 3, and point 7 also exceeds point 5 by a relatively narrow margin, although the rise from point 6 to point 7 has usually been of intermediate scope. The basic advance has normally run from point 1 to point 7, and ends there. The basic advance has continued past point 7 only when there is a definite reason for it. It has ended at point 3 only under unusual circumstances, such as 1943. This was because the decline from point 2 to point A lasted an extremely long time—over nine months.

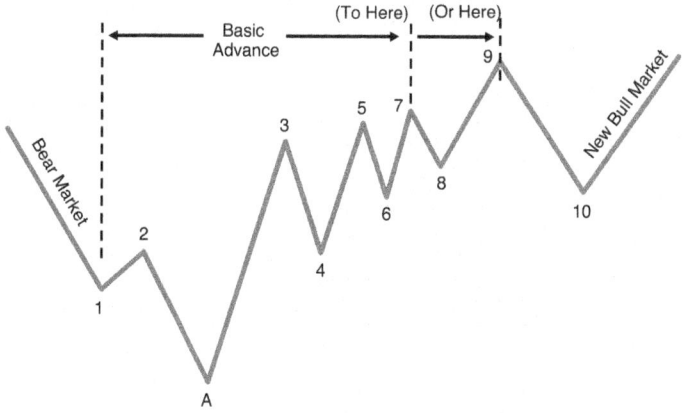

FIGURE 12.2   *Secondary low.*

Point 1	Point A	Point 3	Point 4	Point 7	Point 9	Point 10
6/11/1913	6/30/1914	12/27/1915	5/4/1916	6/12/1916	11/21/1916	12/19/1917
12/21/1920	8/24/1921	6/2/1922	6/12/1922	3/20/1923	[2] 2/6/1924	5/20/1924
6/2/1931	7/8/1932	[1] 7/18/1933	10/21/1933	2/5/1934	none	3/14/1935
5/1/1941	4/28/1942	7/14/1943	11/30/1943	3/13/1944	7/10/1944	9/14/1944
1/30/1970	5/26/1970	4/28/1971	11/23/1971	8/22/1972	1/11/1973	6/26/1973

[1] Point 3 did not exceed point 2.
[2] Point 9 did not exceed point 7.

In all of Lindsay's examples, point 10 lies after a long basic decline (1 year, 1–2 months) after a previous high in his sequence. Those tops are not limited to point 9 but include points 3, 5, 7, and 9.

"I consider the action in 1923-1924 as the most typical example of what the 9 to 10 movement should be...." Figure 12.3 shows stocks dropped 414 days or 13½ months (a typical long basic decline) after the November 3, 1919, bull market top to bottom on December 21, 1920, at point 1. Stocks had to rally and they did, for more than 4 months—longer than they usually do during the course of a single basic decline. Finally, they sank to a new low in August 1921 (point A), decisively under the low of December 1920. The market high, at point 7, was a perfect basic long advance as it counted 819 days from the secondary low at point 1. The drop from point 7 to point 10 was another long basic decline counting 420 days. Note that the basic advance of 819 days is marginally longer than Lindsay's estimate of 775–805 days following a secondary low that occurs before a final low.

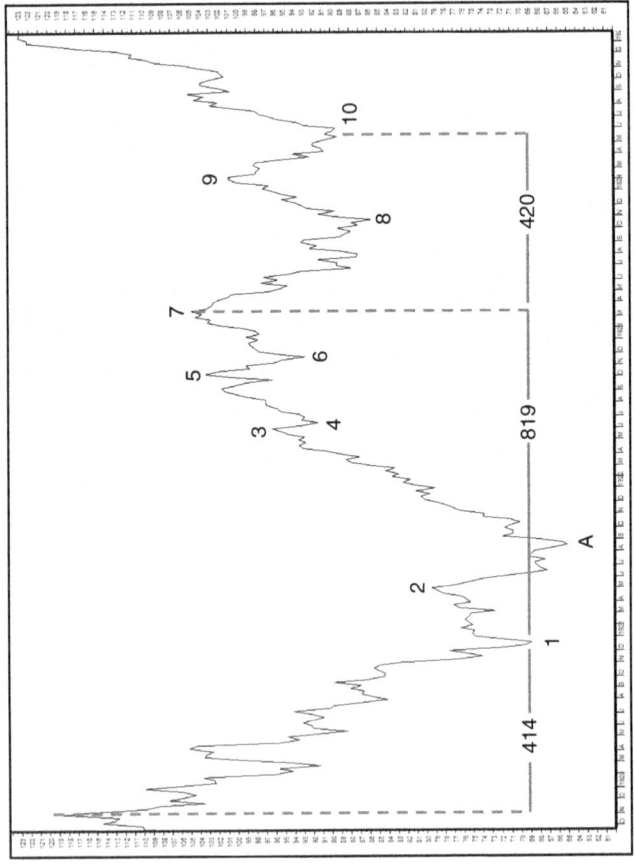

FIGURE 12.3 Secondary low. Chart created by MetaStock®.

Sideways Movements

Occasionally, an advance ends at the appointed time, but there is an interim period before the next decline sets in. This is an intervening period when the theoretical trend is neither up nor down. Lindsay called the market action during this theoretically neutral period a sideways movement. During this time period, the overall result of price movement is approximately sideways—regardless of what price may do in the interim. A sideways period may be thought of as *"a pause in the action while the market is regrouping for the next sustained trend."* A sideways movement may be better described as "extra time" that must be sandwiched in while the average fluctuates back and forth while waiting for the right moment when a continuous trend can begin. This is the chief way in which the Principle of Continuity is interrupted.

Sideways movements have almost always occurred at a top. A sideways movement starts with a break, a rather sharp one in nearly every case. Then there is a recovery back to the approximate level of the old high. Sometimes the average falls short of the high and sometimes it exceeds it. This is not important. Eleven months has been the maximum duration of sideways movements. There have been shorter ones. It is usually best to start counting the next basic decline (not the 12-year interval) from the top of the last rally in a sideways movement. Examples of sideways movements can be found in Table 12.3.

TABLE 12.3 *Sideways Movements*

	Short	Long
11/12/1879–9/27/1880		320
11/19/1885–12/3/1888		379
4/3/1899–9/5/1899	155	
1/19/1906–9/17/1906	241	
1/19/1906–12/11/1906		323
12/27/1915–11/21/1916	330	
2/11/1926–1/25/1927		348
9/3/1929–4/17/1930	227	
2/5/1934–7/26/1934	171	
4/6/1956–8/2/1956	118	
5/14/1965–2/9/1966		271

Table 12.3 is not meant to be a complete record of all sideways movements during this time period. This table is a collection of time spans found throughout Lindsay's writing. Some time spans appear to have been altered slightly by Lindsay as time passed.

Prior to 1910, the rail average is quoted. After that date, the Dow Jones Industrials is used.

Prior to 1885, Lindsay used an index of seven market leaders that he computed from 1861 on, although there were gaps in it.

Lindsay wrote that, since 1842, there had been 40 basic advances. Of these, 31 were followed by recognizable basic declines and 5 were followed by sideways movements. There have also been several minor sideways movements.

Important Rule: The basic decline following a sideways movement begins at the very end of the movement, regardless of whether that was the highest point. But when we count a 12-year interval from a sideways movement, it always begins from the highest point, no matter where it is located.

It is essential to know when there will be a sideways movement. The long-term intervals are the best guide. Following the bull market high of December 3, 1968, the Dow dropped for 14 months until January 30, 1970 (see Figure 12.4). This was the key point from which to count even though the Dow rallied for 2 months after that, until April, and then continued declining until arriving at a lower low on May 26th.

The next important high was expected somewhere between March 14th and April 14, 1972, 775–805 days after the January 30th secondary low. As it was, the high was 4 days late on April 18th.

The way in which the short- and long-term segments of time fit together suggested that there was to be a sideways movement in 1972. Counting the 15-year interval forward from the low of October 22, 1957, targets a period between October 23, 1972 (15 years) and September 22, 1973 (15 years, 11 months). Our rule of thumb count, 15 years, 2 months, targets December 22, 1972, and the actual high was printed on January 11, 1973—15 years, 2 months, and 20 days after the 1957 low.

Moving Upward Out of a Sideways Movement

"Only twice in history—in 1880 and in 1927—has a basic advance started upward at the end of a major sideways movement. On both occasions, it was followed by a drastic bear market, each one consisting of two complete Basic Declines, which followed one another with only a brief rally in between."

184 *George Lindsay and the Art of Technical Analysis*

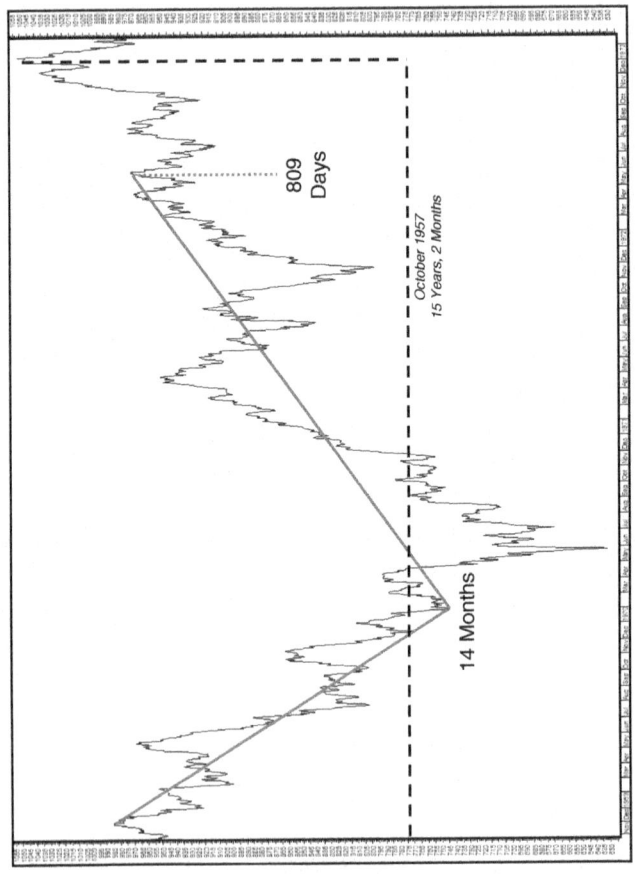

FIGURE 12.4 *Sideways movement. Chart created by MetaStock®.*

Normally the market declines after a sideways movement. Only twice in history has a new basic advance begun at the end of one. It was the formation in 1926 that inspired Lindsay with the concept of the "sideways movement." The break in February and March of that year was much too short to constitute a basic decline.

The first time was 1880; the market had risen to a basic high on November 12, 1879, and then moved sideways until October 11, 1880, when stocks were still below the 1879 top. The market then moved upward from the sideways movement and the bull market high was printed on May 26, 1881. But the basic advance did not end until September 14, 1882, when many market leaders made new highs. This was 704 days after the end of the sideways movement—the typical duration of a short basic advance.

"My index of seven market leaders then declined until 1/21/1884, making the downtrend last 494 days, the longest Basic Decline on record. Until 1927, this was the only case when a Basic Advance began at the end of a Sideways Movement."

Bear in mind that it was the sideways movements of 1880 and 1926 that hinted at what lay ahead. Disaster looms when a basic advance starts at the end of a sideways movement that lasts 11 months.

Conclusion

The following is a quick summary of this chapter and can serve as a quick reference guide in the future for the reader:

The Rule of Continuity states when a downtrend ends—either a basic decline or a long-term interval—an uptrend **of the same class** must begin immediately, and vice versa.

Basic declines have a tendency to include two rallies in succession in roughly the same price range.

After an extended advance (lasting from 929 to 968 days), the basic decline does not begin immediately. If the distance between the Head and the Right Shoulder is more than five months, the whole decline has normally been very long.

The decline is counted from the Head when the elapsed time between the Head and the Right Shoulder is about **five months or less.** When the elapsed time from the Head to the Right Shoulder is more than five months, the probability is that we should count the next basic decline from the Right Shoulder.

There is usually an obvious low between 13 and 14 months after the bull market high.

Every time the 13/14-month low has occurred prior to the ultimate bottom, the length of the following long basic advance has varied between 775 and 805 days.

Once a Basic Movement (advance or decline) persists for longer than the extreme of that particular Standard Time Span, it should be assumed that it will continue until the next time span.

Eleven months has been the maximum duration of sideways movements.

Twelve-year intervals count from highs even in sideways movements.

It is usually best to start counting the next basic decline from the last rally in a sideways movement.

Disaster looms when a basic advance starts at the end of a sideways movement that lasts 11 months.

Endnote

1. Unless otherwise indicated, all quotes in this chapter are taken from George Lindsay's self-published newsletter, *George Lindsay's Opinion,* during the years 1959–72.

Chapter 13

Counts from the Middle Section

"The first original idea I ever had on the stock market remains the best. In 1950, I published a copyrighted pamphlet 'An Aid to Timing' which introduced the concept of the 'Middle Section.' The pamphlet sold well and I received so many letters that I was encouraged to start a market letter of my own the following year on a capital of $600. Since I have never been a big advertiser, it is remarkable that I have lasted in the business for 23 years. I could never have done it without this method. In all the years since then, I have mentioned the principle [of the Middle Section] only once in my advisory letter. Counts from the Middle Section are my prize way of calculating time in the market."[1] –George Lindsay

Nearly every major advance in the stock market has a "Middle Section." This method has been traced back to 1861. The majority of Middle Sections (Ascending and Declining) have continued for 20 weeks or even more. But there have been short Middle Sections in the past, too, especially when they are used to project a low.

A Middle Section is defined by two reactions that interrupt the uptrend. In Figures 13.1 and 13.2 (Lindsay referred to these as "typical schemes"), these two declines are marked as point B to D and from point G to H. In between the two reactions are several smaller rallies. There must be at least two of them, and there may be more.

One prime requirement of a Middle Section is that the overall pace—the rate of gain during the advance—must slow during the course of these small rallies. The slope of the trendline must decrease during a Middle Section as compared to what it was before and after. During a Middle Section the market must gain less ground than it did between points A and B and between points H and J. The whole movement from A to J is a "basic advance."

Point B is the top of an important advance. The average usually spends several days making a minor top formation. Point C is the *"first really weak day after a top."* On this day, the average usually falls cleanly under the low of the minor top formation to form a bottom at point D. During the following advance, the three rallies (E, F, and G) need to be clearly demarcated from one another. Point G is the last rally, point F is the next-to-the-last rally, and point E is the second-to-the-last rally. The decline from point G to point H (in an Ascending Middle Section) is typically longer than the reaction following point F. It can become a Descending Middle Section in its own right, provided that it contains two rallies at about the same price level on the way down. Point H is the end of the Middle Section. Point J may or may not be the top of a complete bull market. Lindsay never indicated if the remaining points in his "typical schemes" held any significance.

When the small rallies within a Middle Section exceed the high at point B, it is called an "Ascending Middle Section," as shown in Figure 13.1. When the small rallies fall short of the level at point B, it is called a "Descending Middle Section," as shown in Figure 13.2.

Note that in a Descending Middle Section, point F becomes a bottom rather than a top as in the Ascending Middle Section. This makes point E the next-to-the-last rally in a Descending Middle Section, rather than the second-to-last rally as in an Ascending Middle Section.

The same basic advance may contain two separate Middle Sections that are entirely disconnected from each other. It doesn't matter whether one is ascending and the other is descending, or whether both are of the same variety. The Middle Section cannot be used to compute the high of the bull market in which it occurs. It must be used to calculate the time of the next bear market low or the high of the bull market after that. These counts are used to target lows and highs far into the future. These counts don't always work but, when they do work, they do so with amazing accuracy.

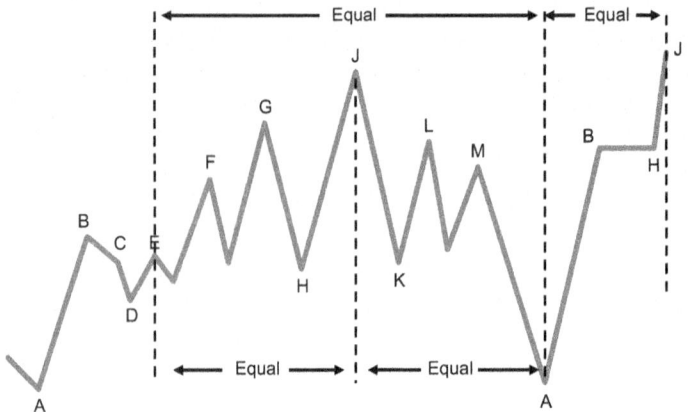

FIGURE 13.1 *Ascending Middle Section.*

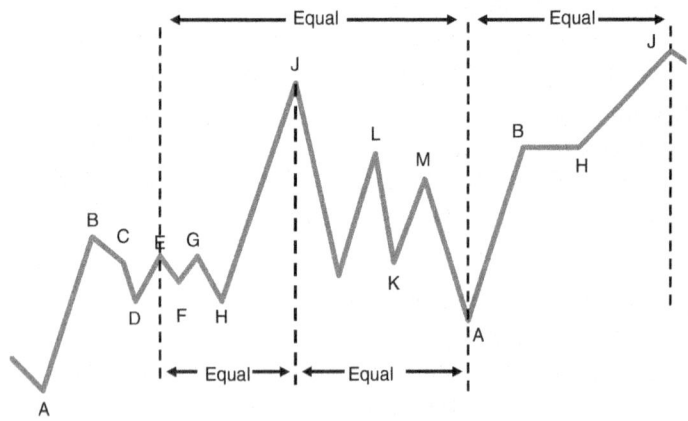

FIGURE 13.2 *Descending Middle Section.*

All counts from Middle Sections are equal distances in time. If the time span originates at a low, the result will be a high. If it originates from a high, the result will be a low. When counting from a Middle Section, counting from either point C or point E is correct, but never both in the same instance. The correct count has originated at point E in the great majority of cases so it always pays to start there. When counting, Lindsay normally used closing prices but he noted that closing, or intraday prices, tend to work equally well. A count from points C or E in a Middle Section must conclude on the absolute high or low of a basic advance or decline; there is no use of secondary lows.

Combining Standard Time Spans with Counts from the Middle Section

"*Whenever an equidistance from a Middle Section has coincided with one of the time spans listed [in Tables 12.1 and 12.2] I have automatically considered that point as the end of the Basic Advance (or Basic Decline).*"

The Standard Time Spans can be used alone, but it is much more accurate to combine them with the counts from the Middle Section and with the long-term intervals. The Standard Time Spans are more reliable than counts from the Middle Section, but the latter, if computed accurately, are much more exact. Both should be used in combination.

The target derived from a count or "equidistance" from point C or E in a Middle Section is valid only if the result falls within the targeted range of one of the Basic Movements. Sometimes, neither the count from point C nor the count from point E in the same Middle Section works at all. In that case, we simply have to rely on the less exact basic advances and basic declines. The Standard Time Spans are often useful, even essential, in deciding whether to count from point C or E in a Middle Section.

Ascending Middle Sections

The break from point B to point D is almost always deeper than the break that terminates at point A. When that is not clear, look for a clearly defined point C. When one rally is much smaller than the others in an Ascending Middle Section, it is almost invariably the first rally of the three (rally E). The break from point G to point H should lose more points than the break following point F. If the advance from point E to point F is an extremely long one, then a decline from point G to point H, which is longer than the break following point F, is very likely to become a Descending Middle Section itself when considered in isolation.

Figure 13.3 shows a daily chart from 1951 and a Middle Section in detail. It is an Ascending Middle Section because point G exceeded the level at point B, the top of the previous sustained advance. In every Middle Section, there are always two possible points from which we count time. One such point is point E. In an Ascending Middle Section, point E is always the second-to-the-last rally. That day was April 6, 1951.

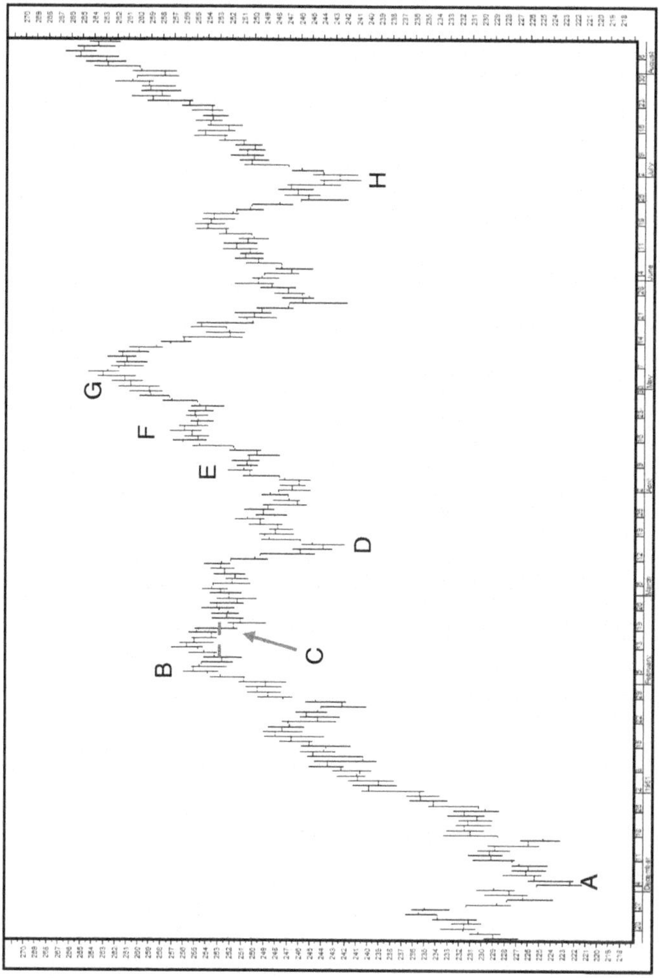

Counts from the Middle Section 195

FIGURE 13.3 *Middle Section, 1951. Chart created by MetaStock®.*

Counting from E to the next important low, September 14, 1953, is 892 days. Referring to the table of basic advances (see Table 12.1), it can be seen that no market advance has ever lasted anything like 892 days. One group of advances has continued from 765 to 830 days, while another has lasted from 929 to 968 days—but nothing in between.

In this case, point C is the other possible measuring point in the Middle Section of 1951. Point B is the top of an important advance. The average usually spends several days making a top formation. In Figure 13.3, point B was February 13, 1951. The Dow held a narrow range for the next four days, creating a minor top formation. The average had a relatively large loss on February 19th and fell cleanly under the low of the minor top formation. This was a perfect example of point C, the first really weak day after a top.

Point C was 938 days before the bear market low in September 1953. Counting forward another 938 days targets Monday, April 9, 1956, as a top for the bull market. The Dow made its intraday bull market high that Monday and its closing high the previous Friday (see Figure 13.4).

Descending Middle Sections

A Descending Middle Section is essentially a downtrend in a long bull market. The downtrend must be interrupted by two small rallies at about the same level and must then continue still lower. When there are three rallies, one of them (usually the last, but it was the first in 1937) is either brief or inconsequential.

Counts from the Middle Section 197

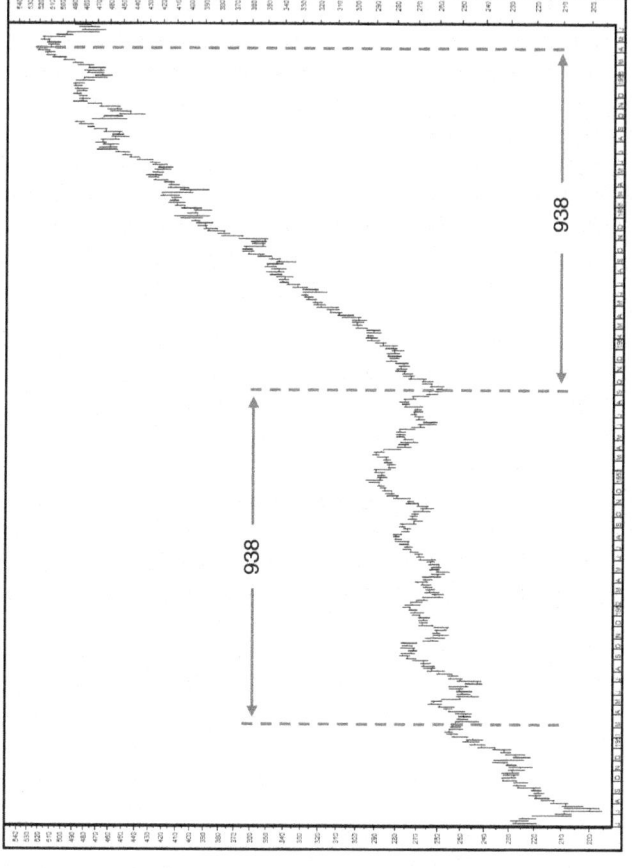

FIGURE 13.4 Middle Section, 1956 market top. Chart created by MetaStock®.

After falling until June 10, 1965, the Dow rose one day, fell one day, and then rose for three days to culminate on June 17th. Two distinct rallies in the same price range, and the average subsequently fell lower (see Figure 13.5). This fulfills the essential requirements of a Descending Middle Section. As a rule, the rallies in a Middle Section last longer but the essential requirement is a sharp break between the two rallies of a Descending Middle Section.

Counting from point E of the Descending Middle Section to the top of the market advance on February 9, 1966, is 243 days. Counting forward another 243 days targets a low on Monday, October 10, 1966 (see Figure 13.6). That Monday was the exact date of the intraday low and the previous Friday was the closing low of the 1966 bear market.

Conclusion

The following is a quick summary of this chapter and can serve as a quick reference guide in the future for the reader:

The overall pace—or the rate of gain during the advance—must slow down during the course of the Middle Section.

Point E is the second-to-the-last rally in an Ascending Middle Section and the next-to-the-last rally in a Descending Middle Section.

The correct count has originated at point E in the great majority of cases, so it always pays to start there.

Counts from the Middle Section 199

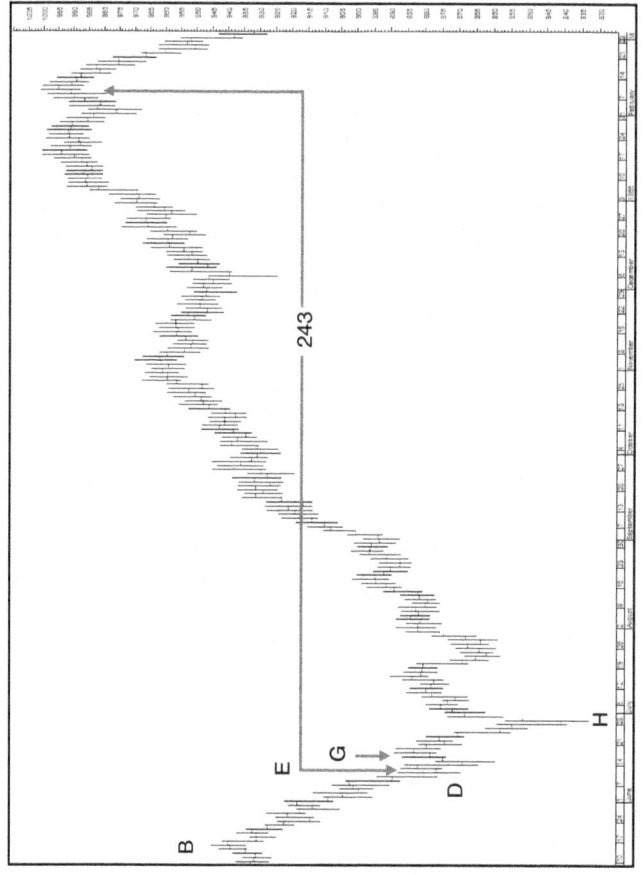

FIGURE 13.5 Descending Middle Section, 1965. Chart created by MetaStock®.

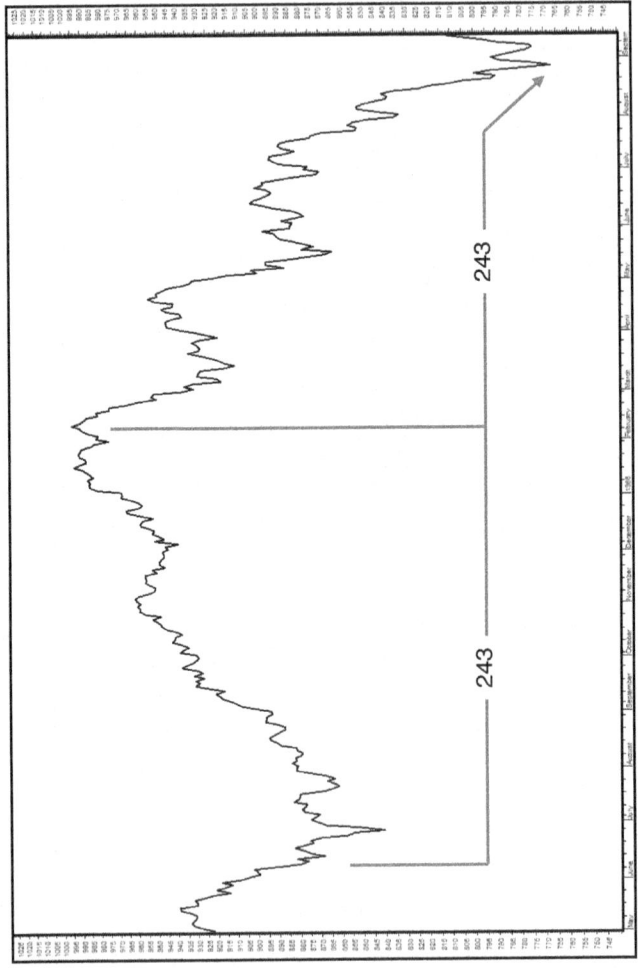

FIGURE 13.6 Descending Middle Section, 1966 market bottom. Chart created by MetaStock®.

Normally, the count from either point C or point E works—but not both of them.

A Descending Middle Section contains two rallies at about the same level prior to the bottom.

In an Ascending Middle Section...

...when one rally is much smaller than the others in an Ascending Middle Section, it is almost invariably E.

...the break from point B to point D is almost always deeper than the break that terminates at point A.

...the break from point G to point H should lose more points than the break following point F.

Endnote

1. Unless otherwise indicated, all quotes in this chapter are taken from George Lindsay's self-published newsletter, *George Lindsay's Opinion*, during the years 1959–72.

Chapter 14

Case Study: The 1960s

"The expiration of the 15-year interval is the point where all the movements even up temporarily. They come into a sort of balance. Even though it won't last, it helps us to look back and find out what has really happened, and it enables us to begin a new series of forecasts."[1] –George Lindsay

Introduction

When the end of a standard basic move and the end of a long-term interval coincide in time, there is a *"decisive and often violent movement"* in the market. This can be seen at several points in time, including the highs of September 1929, March 1937, and December 1968, and the lows of July 1932 and June 1949. In this case study, and final chapter of the book, a single decade is examined with the intent of illustrating the concepts covered in previous chapters.

1960–61 Advance

It would have been nice if the decade had started with something more traditional, but instead it chose to begin with two anomalies: a subnormal advance that is quite unusual and a time period (August 1959 to December 1961) that Lindsay considered an example of a 3PDh pattern taking the place of a bear market. The analysis starts with the longer-term counts as it should.

The 15-year interval from the October 1946 low implied that we should have looked for a high sometime between December 1961 and February 1962. In hindsight, we can see that the **November** 1961 (intraday) high counts 15 years, 1 month from the October 1946 low and 8 years, 2 months from the September 1953 low. The **December** 1961 (closing) high, of course, counts to 1 month later.

But when looking for a medium-term interval of about two years, a wide discrepancy is found. The current bull market had begun October 25, 1960. Even if the advance were to be of the minimum duration, 610 days, the high wouldn't come until June 1962 at the earliest.

Counting the basic advance from October 25, 1960, to the intraday high on November 15, 1961, is only 386 days—an irregular advance. The same is true if the count is taken to the closing high on December 13th. There have been only three genuine advances that have been subnormal: those of 1932–34, 1946–48, and 1960–61. To sum up the matter: Most market movements have always followed the Standard Time Spans:

short, mean, long, extended. A few movements have not, and then the timing norms are worthless. But in these cases, you have the shape of the moves on a chart to go by. When a 3PDh appears, act according to its shape, not the number of days.

The 1961 high was an almost unique case. Finding the top was not problematic, however, as the time period from August 1959 to December 1961 unfolded as a Three Peaks and a Domed House pattern (see Figure 14.1). When you look at the chart of the period from August 1959 to December 1961, it is hard not to recognize the shape of the 3PDh. A pattern of this kind can simply take the place of a regular advance. In order to target the top of the pattern with the 221- to 224-day count, in this case it must be counted from the top of the First Floor Roof. From May 19, 1961, to December 13, 1961, counts 208 days, 13 days short of the typical count. While not unprecedented, counting from the First Floor Roof is unusual.

A 107-day Top-To-Top count starts August 24, 1961, and counts 111 days to the December 13th top—well within the ±5-day window surrounding the target date 4 days earlier (see Figure 14.2). A minor Low-Low-High interval of 13 days stretches from the lows of November 17th to November 30th and on to the high of December 13th. A major Low-Low-High interval can be counted using the major low of December 5, 1960, and the minor low of May 26, 1961. They count 171 days to Sunday, November 12, 1961—3 days off from the alternate high of November 15, 1961 (see Figure 14.1).

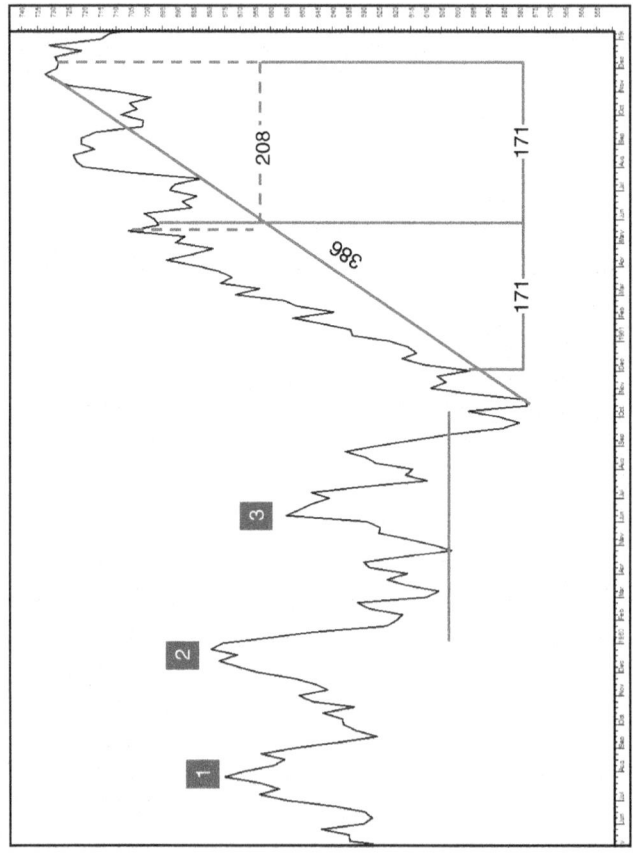

FIGURE 14.1 1960–61 advance 3PDh. Chart created by MetaStock®.

Case Study: The 1960s 207

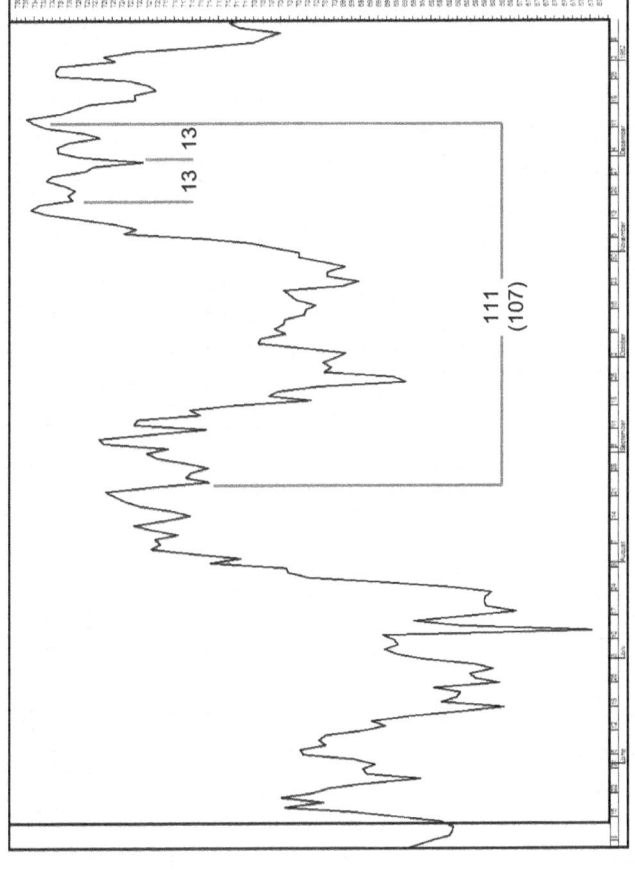

FIGURE 14.2 *1960–61 advance Lindsay Timing Model. Chart created by MetaStock®.*

1961–62 Decline

The drop from December 1961 to the market low in June 1962 was only 194 days—too short to constitute a basic decline, so we look for a secondary low that often follows such a break (see Figure 14.3). It came on October 23, 1962. It was higher than the June low and only 10 months after the high (not the 13–14 months that we normally expect), but that doesn't matter. The secondary low of October 23, 1962, came 314 days after the December high—barely enough time to qualify as a short basic decline. Sometimes it is more accurate to use intraday figures than closing prices. The intraday high came on November 15, 1961. From there, the low in October came an ideal 342 days later. So, the decline of 1961–62 is considered as having ended in October 1962 and the next basic advance must begin on the same day. The 12-year interval counts 12 years, 4 months from the high of June 1948 to October 1962.

1962–66 Advance

When the Dow started up on October 23, 1962, it was known, from the Principle of Alternation, that the advance would be long because the previous advance (October 1960–November/December 1961) had been a short basic advance. What wasn't known is if it would be extended. If the advance had been merely long, it would have lasted until December 1964 (2 years, 2 months).

Case Study: The 1960s 209

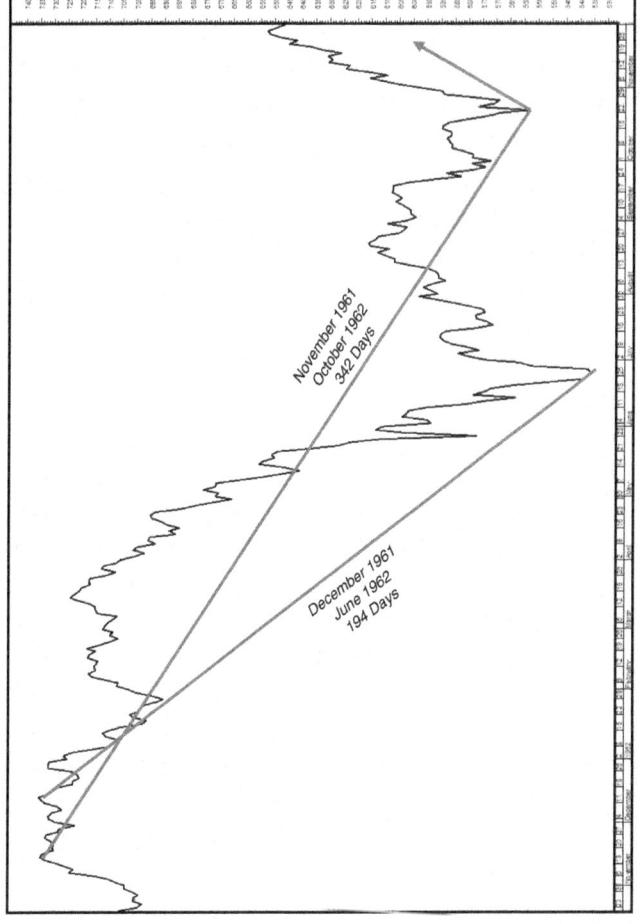

FIGURE 14.3 1961–62 decline. Chart created by MetaStock®.

Note the 12-year interval starting at the high of January 1953. It called for a low sometime between March (12 years, 2 months) and September (12 years, 8 months) 1965. Taking full advantage of the time span and counting to September 1965 would still mean a decline of only about 8 months from a possible high the previous December. That would have been barely long enough for a subnormal basic decline.

In **this scenario,** a new basic advance would then begin in September 1965. Looking ahead, the end of the next 15-year interval from September 1953 targeted a major top toward the end of 1968 (rule of thumb: 15 years, 2 months). If a basic advance began in September 1965, it would need to run for 3 years, 3 months. That time span is much too long for a basic advance using the Standard Time Spans.

The market continued to advance through December, and by mid-May 1965, the advance from the low of October 1962 had endured for 934 days. That is just about the maximum duration of an extended basic advance. No advance has ever exceeded the limit of 929 to 968 days. The advance had to end soon, yet, other than an interim correction, a full-fledged bear market was not in the cards. With the 12-year low mentioned previously, expected no later than September 1st, any decline beginning the previous May could therefore last only about 110 days. That isn't nearly long enough to constitute a basic decline.

Another problem is that any advance that begins in response to a 12-year interval usually lasts seven months **or longer,** and that's what happened here. Seven months is too long for a rally in a bear market that, **in this scenario,** was to have started in May 1965.

The only other alternative is that the latter part of 1965 will be a sideways movement. The 12-year low actually came at the end of June 1965. Seven months from late June 1965 places the final high at about the end of January 1966. The bull market ended in February 1966, and that was the end of the sideways movement (see Figure 14.4). The high in February 1966 was higher than it had been in May 1965 when the sideways movement started. It doesn't matter. The highest point of a sideways movement may come at the start, in the middle, or at the end. The trend is suspended during a sideways movement. It resumes as soon as it ends.

Another way of targeting the February 1966 top is a 3PDh that extended from late 1964 to the top on February 9, 1966 (see Figure 14.4). The three peaks are seen in November 1964, February 1965, and May 1965. Peak 3 even breaks down into a fractal of a complete 3PDh formation. With the major 3PDh having a nonsymmetrical base, the 221- to 224-day count originates at the bottom of the Separating Decline, June 28th, and counts 226 days to the February high.

The February 9th high to the bull market was an exact 107 days from the key date of October 25, 1965, a dip prior to a top. The 107-day interval count is confirmed by a major LLH interval consisting of 101 days from July 22, 1965, to November 1, 1965. Counting forward another 101 days targets February 9, 1966. Another major LLH interval originates at the bottom of the reaction from Peak 1 and counts 227 days to the bottom of the Separating Decline. Counting from there to the bull market high was 226 days.

212 George Lindsay and the Art of Technical Analysis

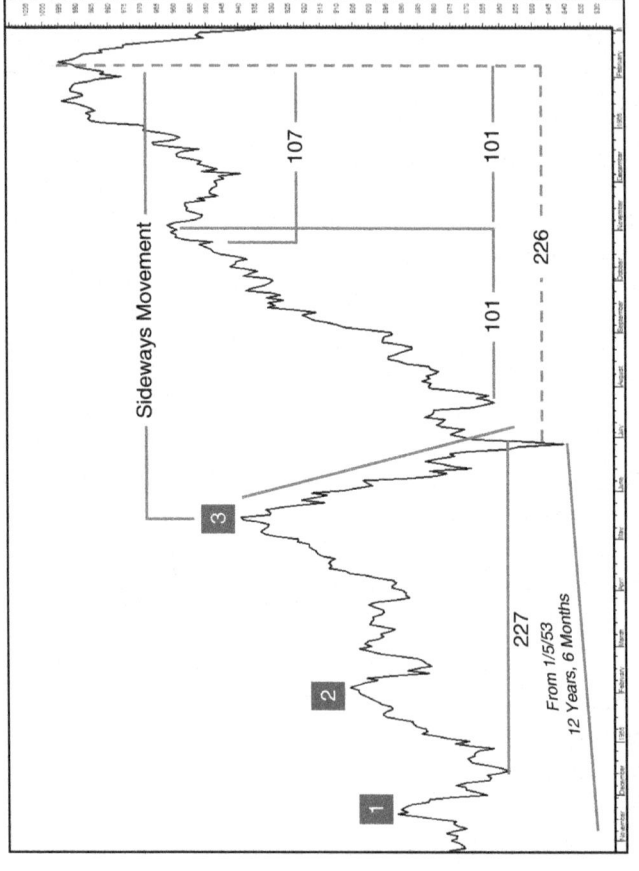

FIGURE 14.4 1962–66 advance. Chart created by MetaStock®.

1966 Decline

After the market top on February 9, 1966, the Dow fell for 97 days to May 17th. This could not be the ultimate bottom of the decline for two important reasons. First, the decline from February to May, at 97 days, was much too short for any of the Standard Time Spans.

Second, the next bull market high was not due until sometime between November 1968 and January 1969. This estimate came from counting 15 years, 2 months and 15 years, 4 months from the September 1953 low. The count from May 1966 to November 1968 was 915 days. That would have put the advance into the "no man's land" between a long (830 days) and an extended (929 days) basic advance.

January would have been 2 years and 8 months, or 976 days. Extended advances can continue for as much as 2 years and 7 months. Note that 976 days is beyond the 968-day limit and, in addition, the market just had an extended advance in 1962–65. Two such advances have never followed one another in succession (Principle of Alternation).

If the decline was to continue, at some point there should be two rallies in succession in roughly the same price range. This decline saw three rallies, rather than two, from the low of May 17th to the high of July 8th (see Figure 14.5). In major bear markets of the past, the two or three rallies have often continued for 15 to 18 weeks. These rallies lasted only 52 days, less than two months. When there are three rallies, one of them (usually the last, but it was the first in 1937) is either brief or inconsequential.

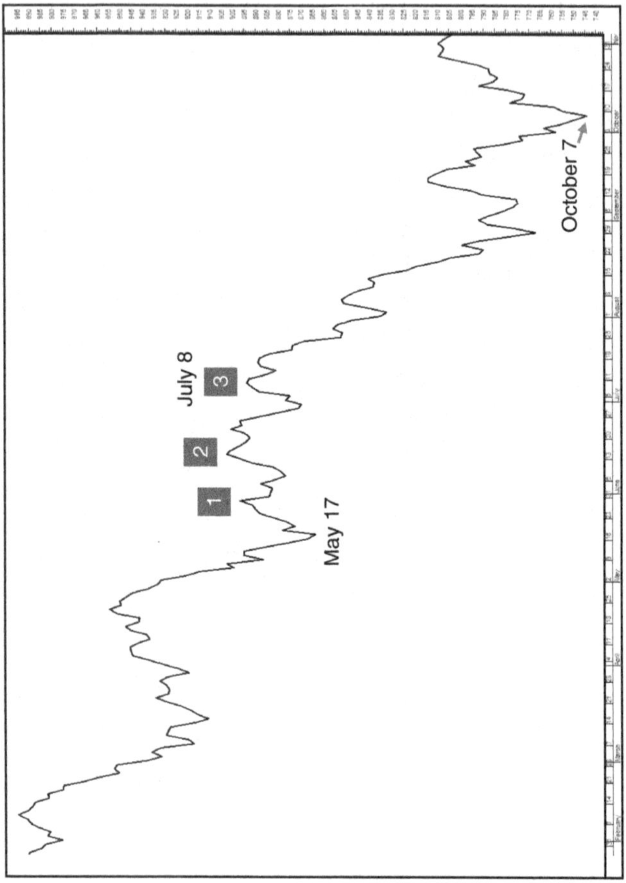

FIGURE 14.5 1966 decline. Chart created by MetaStock®.

The decline from February 9, 1966, to October 7, 1966, was subnormal as it lasted only 239 days. The brevity of the three rallies was a hint, but not conclusive evidence, that the decline would be shorter than usual.

There was another, more specific way to time the basic low in late 1966, however. Looking all the way back to 1965, the Dow fell from May 14th to June 10th. The Dow then rose one day (June 11th), fell one day, and then rose for three days to culminate on June 17th. Two distinct rallies in the same price range, and the average subsequently fell lower. This fulfills the essential requirements of a Descending Middle Section. As a rule, the rallies in a Middle Section last longer, but the essential requirement is a sharp break between the two rallies of a Descending Middle Section. This is the same Descending Middle Section that was examined in Chapter 13, "Counts from the Middle Section," so it won't be repeated here except to add that this Middle Section also functions as the Separating Decline in the 3PDh mentioned in the earlier discussion of the 1962–66 advance (see Figure 14.4).

1966–68 Advance

Returning to the long-term interval count from the major low on September 14, 1953, this count targets a high in the vicinity of November 1968, 15 years, 2 months later. Remember: The 15-year interval stretches from 15 years to 15 years, 11 months.

There had been another important low on October 25, 1960. Counting 8 years forward targets 1968. This count places a high between October and December 1968 (8 years to 8 years, 2 months). The two long-term counts coincide, and the very fact that they agreed so closely increased the probabilities of a severe decline (see Figure 14.6).

To time the top more closely, refer to the medium-term interval of about 2 years and the bear market low of October 7, 1966. Count the typical duration of a long advance, 775–805 days. This placed the probable time of the top somewhere between November 21 and December 21, 1968 (see Figure 14.7). The bear market low in October 1966 did not begin at a 12-year interval where nearly all major advances have taken off. The year 1966 was not 12 years after any important top. The gain from 1966 to 1968 was therefore only a minor bull market in terms of the Dow Industrials.

A 3PDh pattern (see Figure 14.8) can also be seen during this period. Peak 1 (May 5, 1967) and Peak 3 (January 8, 1968) are eight months apart. The First Floor Wall takes place March through May 1968 and even has the initial false pullback in April that is fairly common. The First Floor Roof has five reversals. The only tricky item here is that in order to get a count of 221–224 days to time the top, it must be counted from that initial false pullback in April—which counts 225 days. Given that the count is only 1 day more than perfect, and it originates at the bottom of a pullback, this suggests that the top would have been caught by the observant (and patient) analyst.

Case Study: The 1960s 217

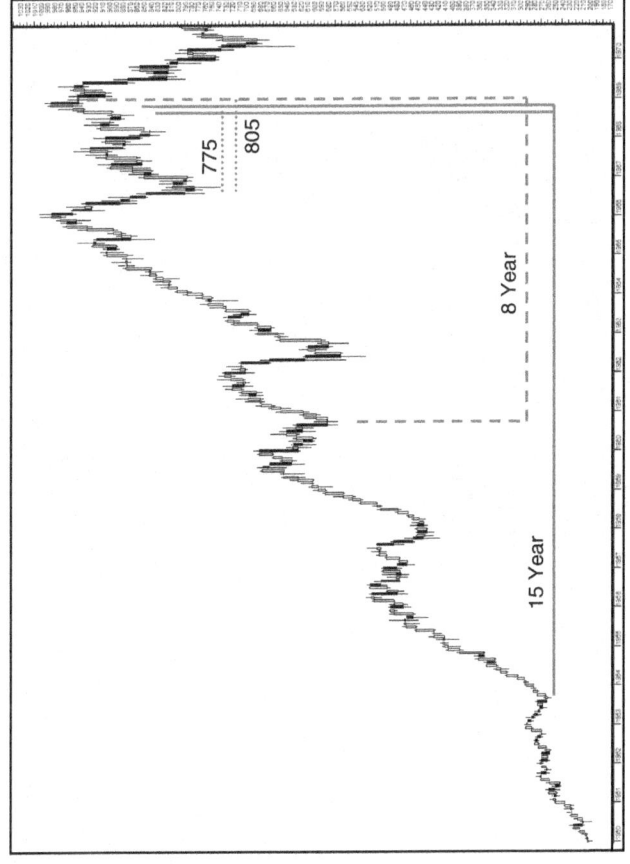

FIGURE 14.6 1966–68 advance: long-term intervals. Chart created by MetaStock®.

218 *George Lindsay and the Art of Technical Analysis*

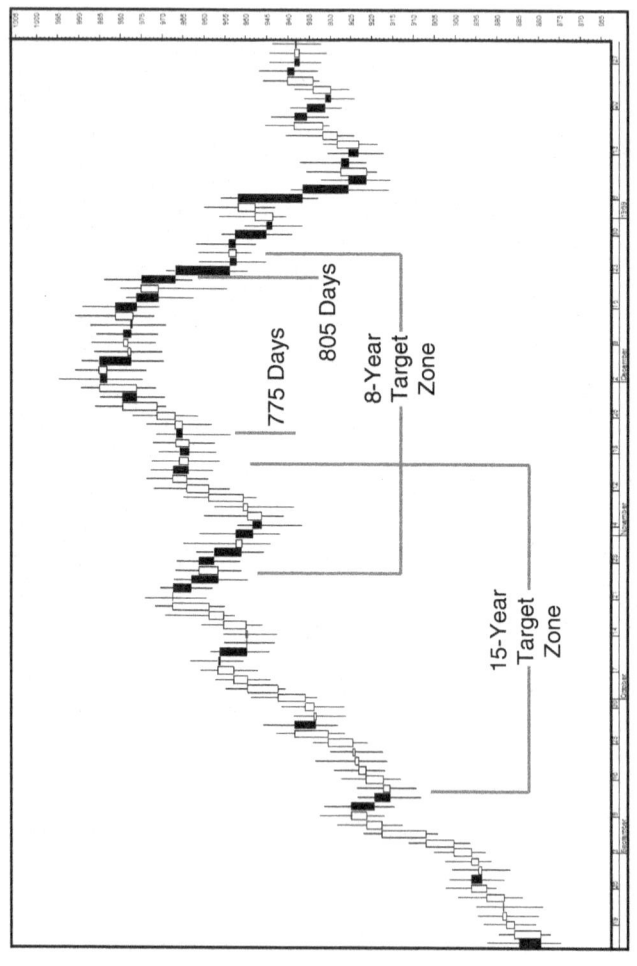

FIGURE 14.7 *1966–68 advance, basic long advance. Chart created by MetaStock®.*

Case Study: The 1960s 219

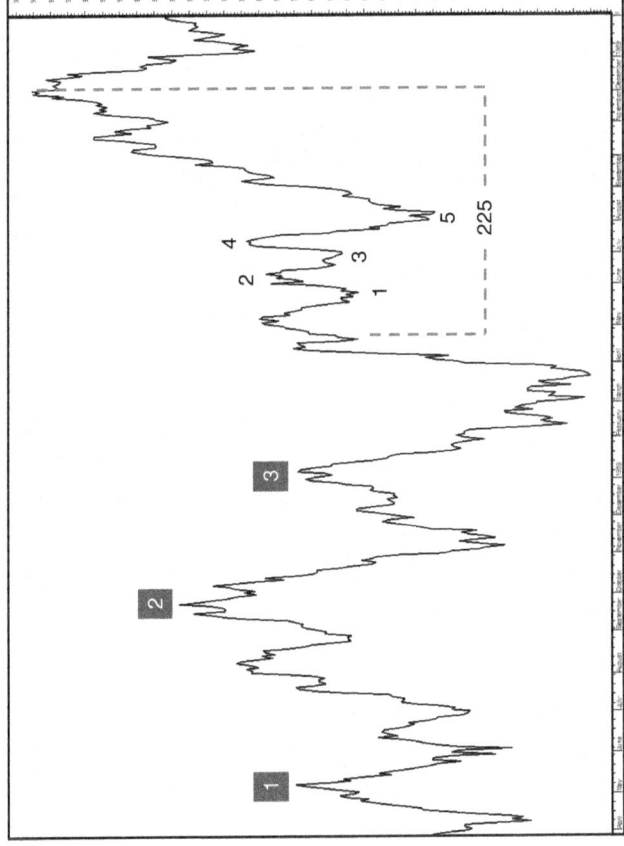

FIGURE 14.8 1966–68 advance: 3PDh pattern. Chart created by MetaStock®.

1968–70 Decline

A low could have been expected in late 1969/early 1970. That is because the 12-year interval from the high of July 12, 1957, placed a low somewhere between September 1969 (12 years, 2 months) and March 1970 (12 years, 8 months). As it turned out, the low arrived 12 years, 10 months later, in May 1970.

Sometime during the decline from December 1968, two rallies in roughly the same price range would be expected to form. The two rallies began on July 29th and lasted until November 10th, 104 days or almost 15 weeks later. The second rally was higher than the top of the first rally. In the majority of cases, the two (or three) rallies make a series of descending tops. The subsequent decline from November 10th to January 30th lasted 82 days and was shorter than most major bear market legs (see Figure 14.9).

January 30, 1970, came 423 days (1 year, 2 months) after a bull market high in December 1968, the typical duration of a long basic decline. Therefore, 14 months after the top, January 30, 1970, becomes a basic low. Unlike 1966, it did not coincide with a bear market low, as the ultimate low came later in May. A basic low that precedes the final bear market low is very important in this system. A new basic advance must be counted from it.

Case Study: The 1960s 221

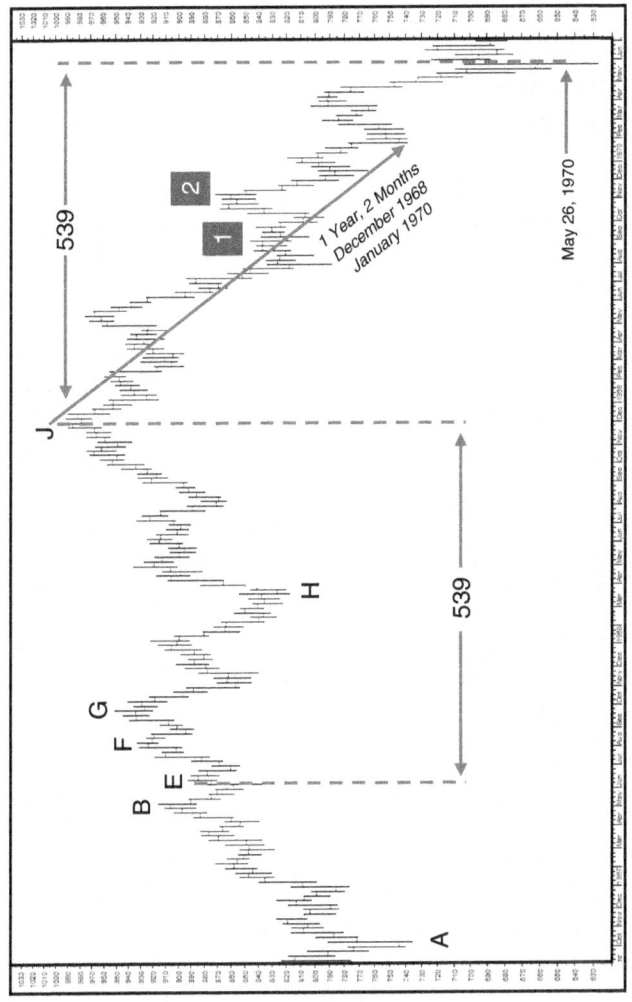

FIGURE 14.9 1968–70 decline. Chart created by MetaStock®.

The fluctuations between B and H in 1967–68 constituted an Ascending Middle Section (see Figure 14.9). Point E fell on June 13, 1967, and counts 539 days until the bull market high on December 3, 1968. Counting 539 days from the December high targets May 26, 1970—the exact date of the bear market low. Note that 539 days is longer than the typical "long" bear market. They have ranged between 386 and 448 days. Declines are more likely to be irregular in their durations than advances. Note that in this example, the date Lindsay labeled with the letter J is a bull market top. Point J isn't always a bull market high.

Before concluding this case study (and this Middle Section), examine the movements between point G and H alone. Ordinarily, they would be merely the second decline in an Ascending Middle Section. But when the decline from G to H contains two rallies at about the same price level, it becomes a Descending Middle Section in its own right.

The decline from point G to H in Figure 14.10 did contain the necessary two rallies, although the dip that separated them was not as sharp as it should have been. This dip was the reaction from December 7th to December 15th. Ideally, prices should have broken under the intraday low posted on December 1st. The demarcation between the two rallies would then have become unmistakable. Nevertheless, the highs of December 7, 1967, and January 9, 1968, must be considered the tops of two separate rallies. December 7th, the high of the next-to-the-last rally, becomes point E. We always count from point E first since it has worked more often than point C.

Case Study: The 1960s 223

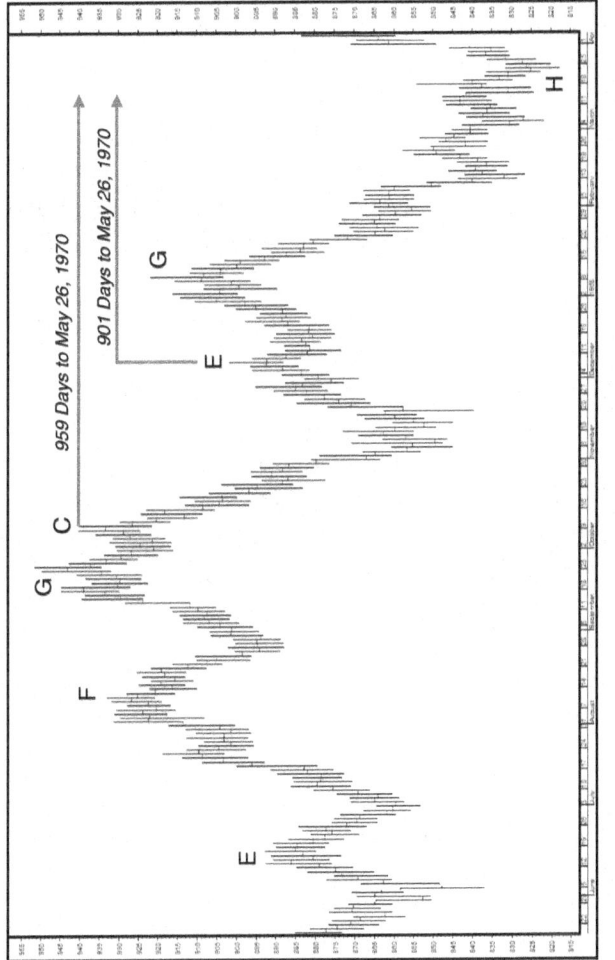

FIGURE 14.10 *Descending Middle Section, 1967-68. Chart created by MetaStock®.*

Counting from point E on December 7, 1967, we find that 901 calendar days elapsed until the bear market low on May 26, 1970 (remember that counts from the Middle Section always center on **absolute** highs and lows and do not use secondary lows). Here is another example of always needing to compare the count from the Middle Section with the Standard Time Spans. In Table 12.1, we found that long advances have continued anywhere from 775 to 830 days, and extended advances have lasted anywhere between 929 and 968 days. But no uptrend since 1877 has ever ended anywhere between 830 and 929 days. Given the historical record, an advance of 901 days was very unlikely.

We abandon point E and go back to point C, the less frequently used measuring point, to see if a count from there will fit better. The Dow formed a small top between September 14, 1967, and October 9, 1967. The first very weak day after the high, October 10th, becomes point C. It was 959 days before the bear market low of May 26, 1970. Counting 959 days forward from there, we arrive at January 9, 1973.

Notice that 959 days fall within the range of extended basic advances as shown in Table 12.1. Early January 1973 was also 15 years and about 2½ months after the bear market low of October 1957. The three ways of counting time coincided as well as they ever do. As it turned out, the bull market high came only two days later than the count from point C indicated it should have—that is, on January 11, 1973.

Conclusion

It is hoped that this case study will help the reader assimilate the material in the preceding chapters. It can be seen that, in the real world, the counts are rarely exactly what Lindsay had prescribed, yet they are surprisingly close, and oftentimes they are exactly as he had written. As noted in the Introduction, it is important to learn the rules and specific counts Lindsay laid out in his years of writing newsletters. Once those guidelines are firmly in mind, you can use them as an anchor from which to drift with the market's ebbs and flows. It is with this footing that you can then declare that you truly have a "feel for the market."

Endnote

1. Unless otherwise indicated, all quotes in this chapter are taken from George Lindsay's self-published newsletter, *George Lindsay's Opinion,* during the years 1959–72.

Glossary

107-Day Interval An interval of 107 calendar days used to forecast the intraday high of an advancing market. The key to using the interval is correctly determining its origin.

Agitation The starting point of a series of time intervals. An agitation may be an episode of violence, eruptions of an emotional nature (religious, economic, or political), or a creative concentration (books, paintings, plays, music, etc.).

Ascending Base A base that forms after the Separating Decline in a Three Peaks and a Domed House pattern. This base is characterized by a series of higher highs and higher lows.

Ascending Middle Section The period in a bull market when the advance slows (relative to what preceded and followed this time period), typically for 20 weeks or more. The formation is used to target tops and bottoms. When the rallies in the middle section exceed the top of the previous advance, it is referred to as an Ascending Middle Section and contains at least three rallies.

Base The base-building phase of a Three Peaks and a Domed House pattern prior to the First Floor Wall.

Basic Advances Different categories of market advances of varying length but all lasting approximately two years.

Basic Declines Different categories of market declines of varying length but all lasting approximately one year.

Basic Movements Either advances or declines composed of the Standard Time Spans.

Bottom to Top Count A possible origin of a 107-day count in the Lindsay Timing Model prior to an extended rise.

Cluster A trading range near, or just after, the expiration of a 107-day count.

Coincident Counts In the Lindsay Timing Model, this is an alignment of a 107-day count with various LLH counts within 24 hours of each other.

Compact Top Formation The common framework of the nine variations of a Key Range.

Count The number of calendar days between the origin and ending of a time interval.

Cupola The top of the Three Peaks and a Domed House pattern that resembles the cupola of a house or head-and-shoulders top.

Descending Base A base that forms after the Separating Decline in a Three Peaks and a Domed House pattern. This base is characterized by a series of lower highs and lower lows.

Descending Middle Section Essentially, a downtrend in a long bull market typically for 20 weeks or more. The formation is used to target tops and bottoms. When the rallies in the middle section fail to exceed the top of the previous advance, it is referred to as a Descending Middle Section and normally contains only two rallies.

Double Bottom Top A Key Range in the Lindsay Timing Model characterized by three highs separated by two lows, the first of which is usually the key date.

Double Top A Key Range in the Lindsay Timing Model characterized by two highs separated by a low that is often the key date.

Extended Advance The longest Basic Advance, varying between 929 and 968 days.

Final Dip A variation of the Key Range concept in the Lindsay Timing Model in which the key date is the final dip in price prior to the high of the advance.

First Floor Roof Often, but not always, a sideways pattern characterized by a five-wave reversal following the First Floor Wall in a Three Peaks and a Domed House pattern.

First Floor Wall A sharp rise following the base in a Three Peaks and a Domed House pattern.

Fractal A geometric shape that can be split into parts, each of which is a reduced-size copy of the whole.

Important Count [1] A count from one important low to another important low not more than two years later. [2] A count from an important low to a minor low not more than three months later.

Important Low During an uptrend, a low in a Low-Low-High interval that drops lower than a previous low in the uptrend preceding the most recent high. An important low can also be a change in trend. Important lows in downtrends precede an upward retracement that climbs higher than a previous upward correction in the same downtrend.

Irregular Base A base that forms after the Separating Decline in a Three Peaks and a Domed House pattern. This base cannot be contained within parallel lines.

Key Date The origin of the 107-day count used in the Lindsay Timing Method.

Key Range The price range within which the key date is located. A Key Range has nine possible variations.

Lindsay Timing Model A timing method used to identify the intraday price high of a market advance using both the 107-day interval and the Low-Low-High interval.

Long Advance A basic advance that varies between 715 and 830 days.

Long Decline A basic decline typically lasting 13 or 14 months.

Long-Term Intervals The elapsed time from an important high to an important low or vice versa. The two low-to-high intervals are approximately 8 years and approximately 15 years. The high-to-low interval lasts approximately 12 years.

Low-Low-High Interval Two price lows separated by an interval of time equal to the interval of time separating the second price low from a succeeding price high.

M-Pattern A series of historic cycles lasting almost 400 years from beginning to end. The pattern describes the expected timing of a nation's good and bad fortune.

Major Top Formation A top formation that extends over several months and normally includes several Compact Top formations.

Medium-Term Intervals Counted in days and referred to as the Standard Time Spans or Basic Movements.

Minor Count [1]A count from one minor low to another minor low. [2]A count from one minor low to an important low. A minor low is valid for no more than four months.

Minor Lows A low in the Low-Low-High interval that is any low other than an "important low."

Post Top Counts A 107-day count in the Lindsay Timing Model taken from a key date **after** the high in a Key Range, rather than the more common approach of a key date **prior to** the high of the Key Range.

Principle of Alternation The principle holds that Basic Movements of the same class and direction alternate in length. A long advance is followed by a short advance.

Principle of Equalization In a Three Peaks and a Domed House pattern, when one formation (the Three Peaks or the Domed House) falls short of the normal duration, the other pattern equalizes the total elapsed time by becoming longer or shorter.

Range Dip Similar to a final dip in the Lindsay Timing Model except that the final dip, rather than being in the Key Range, is the final dip **prior to** the Key Range.

Retrograde Movement An attempt to change the course of events in history that usually occurs before the expiration of the 40-year interval in Lindsay's Technical History and serves to confuse the outlook.

Rule of Continuity When a long-term or medium-term trend ends, an opposite trend, of the same class, must begin immediately.

Second Floor Wall A sharp rise following the First Floor Roof in a Three Peaks and a Domed House pattern.

Secondary Low A temporary bottom in a decline that occurs 13–14 months after a high in the market.

Separating Decline The sell-off following the third peak in a Three Peaks and a Domed House pattern. The decline must terminate at a point below at least one of the reactions following peaks one or two.

Short Advance A basic advance of less than two years.

Short Decline A basic decline typically varying between 340 and 355 days.

Short-Term Intervals The counts in the Three Peaks and a Domed House and Lindsay Timing Models.

Sideways Movement An intervening period when the theoretical trend is neither up nor down.

Sinking Key Range A Key Range in the Lindsay Timing Model that appears as a consolidation in a declining market.

Special Class A key date in the Lindsay Timing Model such as a dip succeeding a Bottom to Top Count. Any 107-day counts originating at such an origin should be expected to target a short-lived bounce in an already existing decline.

Standard Time Spans The various durations of market moves that have recurred throughout history.

Subnormal Advance An extremely short and relatively rare basic advance.

Subnormal Decline An extremely short basic decline varying between 222 and 250 days.

Swingover In the Tri-Day Method a ratio found by dividing the distance from the bottom of the Separating Decline to the top of the Domed House by the distance from Peak Three to the bottom of the Separating Decline.

Symmetrical Base A base that forms after the Separating Decline in a Three Peaks and a Domed House pattern. This base can be contained within parallel lines.

Target Date The 107th calendar day after the key date in the Lindsay Timing Model.

Technical History The term Lindsay used to describe the methods in his book *The Other History*.

Three Peaks and a Domed House A geometric pattern used to find the end of a bull market.

Top-to-Top Count A method using the 107-day interval to target the top of a market advance.

Tri-Day Method A series of calculations to determine a price target for a bottom after the top of a Three Peaks and a Domed House pattern.

True Date The actual intraday high of an advance normally contained within a ±5-day window surrounding the Target Date in the Lindsay Timing Model.

INDEX

Numbers

3PDh (Three Peaks and a Domed House), 47
8-year intervals, 155-159
12-year intervals, 152, 159
15-year intervals, 149-150, 158
107-day counts, combining with LLH (Low-Low-High Count), 124-125
107-day intervals, Lindsay Timing Model, 100
107-Day Top-to-Top count, 95
1960s case study
　1960-1961 advance, 204-205
　1961-1962 decline, 208
　1962-1966 advance, 208-211
　1966 decline, 213-215
　1966-1968 advance, 215-216
　1968-1970 decline, 220-224

A

Adams, Brooks, 24
Adams, Henry, 24
The Advisor, 16
advisory service, 16
agitation, 25
　Creative Concentration, 31-32
　emotional, 29-31
　unsuccessful revolts, 26-28
"An Aid to Thinking," 12
Alphier, James, 16, 18
American Civil War, 26
analyst, 13-14
appearance of George Lindsay, 14
artist, 9-10
Ascending Middle Section, 191, 194-196

B

bases
  Domed House formation, 60-61
  Symmetrical Base, 62
  longer-than-normal Domed House, 66
basic advances, 163-166
  declines following extended basic advances, 171-174
  extended basic advances, 164
  long basic advances, 164
  short basic advances, 164
basic declines, 166-170
Basic Movements, 161
  basic advances, 163-166
  basic declines, 166-170
  long-term intervals, 171
  secondary low sequence, 176, 179
  secondary lows, 174-176
  sideways movements, 181-183
    moving upward out of, 183-185
  Standard Time Spans, 162-163
bear markets, 48
Bottom to Top Counts (BTC), 111
Brown, John, 16-18
BTC (Bottom to Top Counts), 111
bull markets, 48
  shorter-than-normal Domed House, 67

C

calculation steps, Tri-Day Method, 81-82
Campaign GM, 15
case study: the 1960s
  1960-1961 advance, 204-205
  1961-1962 decline, 208
  1962-1966 advance, 208-211
  1966 decline, 213-215
  1966-1968 advance, 215-216
  1968-1970 decline, 220-224
characteristics
  identifying in Three Peaks and a Domed House, 42-47
  of Three Peaks formations, 50-51, 54
Chicago Board of Trade, 10
Christian church, founding, 29
Clusters, 133-136
Coincident Counts, 130-133
Compact Top formations, 105-106
  BTC (Bottom to Top Counts), 111
  Clusters, 134
  Double Bottom Top formations, 107
  Double Top formations, 106

Final Dip, 109-110
Head-and-Shoulders Top
    formations, 108
PTC (Post Top Counts),
    113-114
Range Dip, 110
Sinking Key Range, 114
Special Class, 112
Complex Arrangement, Tri-Day
    Method, 86-89
counts
    Coincident Counts, 130-133
    Domed House formation,
        62-64
    expiring, 130
    important counts, LLH (Low-
        Low-High Count), 123
    LLH (Low-Low-High Count),
        122, 137
    medium-term counts, 161
    Middle Section, 189, 192
        Standard Time Spans,
            193-194
    minor counts, LLH (Low-
        Low-High Count), 123
Creative Concentration, 31-32
Cupola, Domed House
    formation, 75-77
cycles, 143
    long-term, 144-148

D

dates, key dates, 103
    Key Range, 104-105
        Compact Top formations,
            105-114
        Major Top formations,
            105, 115-116
death of George Lindsay, 20
declines, 166-170
    Domed House formation,
        75-77
    expected size of LLH
        (Low-Low-High Count),
        125-126
    following extended basic
        advances, 171-174
Descending Middle Section, 191,
    196-198
difficult to easy, 26
Domed House formation,
    48, 59, 77
    bases, 60-61
    counts, 62-64
    Cupola and the decline, 75-77
    First Floor Roof, 70
        false starts, 74
        missing roofs, 72
        roof rallies, 71-72
    First Floor Wall, 69-70
    longer-than-normal, 64
        descending bases, 66
        short bases, 66

Second Floor Wall, 74
   shorter than normal, 67
Double Bottom Top
   formations, 107
Double Top formations, 106
Douglas Aircraft, 12

E

easy to difficult, 28
Einstein, Albert, 32
Elliott, R. N., 1
emotional agitations, 29-31
Enlightenment, Creative
   Concentration, 32
Esty, William, 10
expiring counts, 130
extended basic advances, 164

F

false starts, First Floor Roof
   Domed House formation, 74
family history of George Lindsay,
   7-8
Final Dip, 109-110
First Floor Roof, 45
   Domed House formation, 70
      false starts, 74
      missing roofs, 72
      roof rallies, 71-72
   missing, shorter-than-normal
      Domed House, 67
First Floor Wall, 45
   Domed House formation,
      69-70
fractals, 54-56
funnel approach, 143

G

George Lindsay's Opinion, 16
Georgel, Gaston, 24
Germany, unsuccessful
   revolts, 28
Granville, Joe, 17-18

H

Head-and-Shoulders Top
   formations, 108
Hirsch, Yale, 13, 18
Hitler, Adolf, 28

I

identifying characteristics, "Three
   Peaks and a Domed House,"
   42-47
important counts, LLH (Low-
   Low-High Count), 123

intervals, 143
  long-term, 146-149, 162
    8-year intervals, 155-159
    12-year intervals, 152, 159
    15-year intervals,
      149-150, 158
    Basic Movements, 171
irregular timing, 3PDh
  ("Three Peaks and a
  Domed House"), 46
irregularities, Three Peaks
  formation, 50-51, 54

K

key dates, 103
  Key Range, 104-105
    Compact Top formations,
      105-114
    Major Top formations,
      105, 115-116
  Key Range, 104-105, 130
    Compact Top formations,
      105-106
      BTC (Bottom to Top
        Counts), 111
      Double Bottom Top
        formation, 107
      Double Top formation,
        106
      Final Dip, 109-110
      Head-and-Shoulders Top
        formation, 108
      PTC (Post Top Counts),
        113-114
      Range Dip, 110
      Sinking Key Range, 114
      Special Class, 112
    Major Top formations, 105,
      115-116

L

Lindsay Sr., George, 8
Lindsay Timing Model, 64,
  93-94, 100
  introduction to, 95-98
  Top-to-Top count, 96
  tops, 99
Lindsay, Albert Loftus, 7
Lindsay, Frank Loftus, 8
Lindsay, George, 1-3
  analyst, 13-14
  artist, 9-10
  death of, 20
  family history, 7-8
Lindsay, Nellie Victoria Meyer, 7
LLH (Low-Low-High Count),
  119-120, 137
  combining with 107-day
    counts, 124-125
  counts, 122
  determining lows, 121-122

expected size of decline,
    125-126
important counts, 123
minor counts, 123
LLH (Low-to-Low-to-High)
    intervals, 103
long basic advances, 164
long basic declines, 167
long-term cycles, 144-148
long-term interval
    12-year intervals, 152, 159
    15-year intervals,
        149-150, 158
    8-year intervals, 155-159
long-term intervals,
    146-149, 162
    Basic Movements, 171
longer-than-normal Domed
    House, 64
    descending bases, 66
    short bases, 66
Los Angeles, 12
lost manuscripts, 33
Low-Low-High Count (LLH),
    119-120, 137
    combining with 107-day
        counts, 124-125
    counts, 122
    determining lows, 121-122
    expected size of decline,
        125-126
    important counts, 123
    minor counts, 123

Low-to-Low-to-High
    intervals, 103
lows
    LLH (Low-Low-High Count),
        121-122
    secondary low sequence,
        176, 179
    secondary lows, 174-176

M

M-Pattern of history, 33
Major Top formations,
    105, 115-116
    Clusters, 133
    trading ranges, 138
McKinley, President, 27
medium-term counts, 161
Middle Section, 189-191
    Ascending Middle Section,
        191-196
    Descending Middle Section,
        191-198
    Standard Time Spans,
        193-194
Middle Sections, counts, 192
minor counts, LLH (Low-Low-
    High Count), 123
minor formations, 54-56
missing roofs, First Floor Roof
    (Domed House
    formation), 72
Model 3, Tri-Day Method, 84-86
moving upward out of sideways
    movements, 183-185

N–O

Nader, Ralph, 15

On Balance Volume indicator, 18
"One Year Later: A Follow-Up of the Three Peaks and Domed House," 40
The Other History, 23

P

Parker, Charlie, 3
patterns at secular bull market tops, shorter-than-normal Domed House, 67
physical appearance, 14
political views, 15-16
Post Top Counts (PTC), 113-114
Principle of Alternation, 170
Principle of Equalization, 47
PTC (Post Top Counts), 113-114

R

Range Dip, 110
retrograde movement, 26
revolts, unsuccessful, 26-28
Right Shoulder, 172
roof rallies, First Floor Roof (Domed House formation), 71-72
rounded effect at the top, 46
Rukeyser, Louis, 19
Rule of Continuity, 162

S

Second Floor Wall, 45
  Domed House formation, 74
secondary low sequence, 176, 179
secondary lows, 174-176
Separating Decline
  Three Peaks formations, 56-57
short basic advances, 164
short basic declines, 166
shorter-than-normal Domed House, 67
sideways movements, 164, 181-183
  moving upward out of, 183-185
Sinking Key Range, 114
Special Class, 112
Special Rule, declines following extended basic advances, 171-174
square effect, 46
Standard Time Spans, 162-163
  Middle Section, 193-194
Stock Trader's Almanac, 18
subnormal, 164
subnormal basic decline, 166-170
Swingover ratio, 80
Symmetrical Base, 62

T

target dates, Lindsay Timing Model, 96
technical history, 23
Teisch, Stuart, 17
terminology, tops, 99
"Three Peaks and a Domed House," 39
  identifying characteristics, 42-47
Three Peaks formation, 49
  characteristics and irregularities, 50-51, 54
  minor formations, 54-56
  Separating Decline, 56-57
time intervals, 25-26
  agitation, 25
A Timing Method for Traders, 93
Timing Model, 64, 93-94, 100
  introduction to, 95-98
  Top-to-Top count, 96
  tops, 99
Top-to-Top count, 125
  Lindsay Timing Model, 96
Top-to-Top counts, 129
Topping Range. *See* Key Range
Topping Ranges, 117
tops, 99
track record, 17, 19
trading ranges, 137-138
Tri-Day Method, 79-80
  calculation steps, 81-82
  Complex Arrangement, 86-89
  Model 3, 84-86
  Swingover ratio, 80

U–V

unsuccessful revolts, 26-28

Victoria, Nellie, 8
violence of fluctuations, 122
von Reichenbach, Stromer, 24

W–X–Y–Z

Wall Street Week, 19-20

Yates, James, 9

In an increasingly competitive world, it is quality of thinking that gives an edge—an idea that opens new doors, a technique that solves a problem, or an insight that simply helps make sense of it all.

We work with leading authors in the various arenas of business and finance to bring cutting-edge thinking and best-learning practices to a global market.

It is our goal to create world-class print publications and electronic products that give readers knowledge and understanding that can then be applied, whether studying or at work.

To find out more about our business products, you can visit us at www.ftpress.com.